Assemble *together* 2

Sixty topical assemblies for secondary schools

Tony Castle

Kevin Mayhew

First published in 2001 by
KEVIN MAYHEW LTD
Buxhall, Stowmarket
Suffolk IP14 3BW

9 8 7 6 5 4 3 2 1 0

ISBN 1 84003 722 9
Catalogue No 1500420

Cover design by Jonathan Stroulger
Edited by Katherine Laidler
Typesetting by Louise Selfe
Printed in Great Britain

Contents

Introduction

Like many another form tutor in a secondary school, I get caught up in planning year·assemblies and form assemblies (our school hall is too small for a whole school assembly) week after week. Like the washing-up and the cleaning at home, it comes around again and again.

It is constantly demanding – if one takes the requirement seriously – to think up new ideas and find fresh material. The pupils live in a world of stimulating presentations, colourful and relevant to their lives. While we cannot – and should not feel that we have to – compete with what our students see and hear in the secular media, there is still a cultural issue. To simply read a passage from the Bible, try to sing a traditional hymn and say the Lord's Prayer may have sufficed in former times, but it will no longer do.

The Christian Faith, and its expression in worship, is of no use to anyone unless it is totally rooted in life and relevant to life. The whole point of Christ is that he is 'Immanuel' (God with us), at one with us in our life experiences.

My first collection, *Assemble Together,* offered material for 60 topical assemblies, which required planning, adequate preparation and some rehearsal. This collection has exactly the same topics, but it is more direct and easy to use. It can be picked up on the very morning of the assembly and used with little preparation. A 'pick and mix' approach is recommended and provision is made for that in the supplementary readings and the suggested alternatives.

One of the major problems that many Christian secondary schools encounter is getting adolescents to sing! This was surmounted, in part, in *Assemble Together* by recommending pop music that they could listen to instead. Here several hymn alternatives are suggested in the hope that one or other of them might be in the school repertoire.

If you would like even more material to supplement the 60 topics here, you will need the first book; they complement each another.

It is my hope that, after using these assemblies for a short while, the user will gain both the enthusiasm and the confidence to abandon the book and only turn to it occasionally as a resource for their own assemblies.

Tony Castle
Lent 2001

Scripture readings

- The Good News Bible or the New International Version are recommended for the Scripture readings.

- There are two books which you may also find useful:
  Winding Quest: The Heart of the Old Testament in Plain English (Oxford University Press, 1972)
  New World: The Heart of the New Testament in Plain English (Oxford University Press, 1967)
  both by Alan T. Dale.

  The aim of these books was to enable ordinary readers – and especially young people – to enjoy and understand the Bible. Unfortunately both are now out of print but many school libraries may still have copies and it would be worth seeking them out. In a few instances, where I felt it was particularly useful, I have included Alan Dale's version; elsewhere I have given a page reference.

Note on suggested hymns

HON   *Hymns Old and New* – all the hymns quoted are included in both of the following editions: *Complete Anglican Hymns Old and New* (Kevin Mayhew, 2000) and *Liturgical Hymns Old and New* (Kevin Mayhew, 1999)

Source   *The Source:* the definitive worship collection compiled by Graham Kendrick (Kevin Mayhew, 1998)

Acknowledgements

The publishers wish to express their gratitude to the following for permission to include copyright material in this book:

The William Barclay Estate for the prayer 'O God, thank you for making me as I am' by William Barclay.

Mrs Rodney Bennett for the poem 'Windy Nights' by Rodney Bennett.

Continuum International, Wellington House, 125 Strand, London, WC2R 0BB, for the extracts from *God'll Fix It* by Jimmy Savile.

Mrs P. E. Dale for the extracts from *Winding Quest* and *New World* by Alan Dale.

Harcourt Inc., 6277 Sea Harbor Drive, 6th Floor, Orlando, Florida 32887-6777, USA, for the excerpt from *The People, Yes* by Carl Sandburg, © 1936 Harcourt Inc., and renewed 1964 by Carl Sandburg. Reprinted by permission of the publisher.

HarperCollins Publishers, 77-85 Fulham Palace Road, Hammersmith, London, W6 8JB, for the extract from *Miracle on the River Kwai* by Ernest Gordon.

Miss Brenda Holloway for the prayer 'Lord Jesus, we are thinking of you in the desert' from *Prayers for Children*, published by Hodder & Stoughton Ltd.

The Merton Legacy Trust, New York, for the quotation by Thomas Merton.

Fr Patrick Sayles for his two prayers 'Lord, if I forget the poor' and 'You are Lord of the poor'.

Rev Robin J. Williamson for 'The Binmen of Belfast' from *Thought for the Day*.

COMMUNITY

A1 Community

HYMN   All people that on earth do dwell (HON/Source)

READING   In America in the 1860s, when covered wagons were heading west, the leaders always dreaded the fording of the River Platte. The current was so changeable in the broad, muddy stream that not even experienced scouts could tell where the pockets of quicksand and potholes lay. When an ox-team got stuck, the wagon was usually overturned, dumping family and possessions into the river. The difficulty was easily overcome. When a large number of wagons had arrived at the river, the oxen from all of them were hitched together in a long line to pull each of the families across in turn. Even though one team in the long line floundered, there were always enough on sure footing to keep the wagon on the move.
Anon

COMMENT   On our own we often feel lost; we feel the need of other people's help and support. Being of help and support to one another is the way God wants it to be.

SCRIPTURE READING   Acts 2:42-47 (or *New World*, page 166)

PRAYER   Almighty God,
we ask you to give your blessing
to this school community.
Help all of us gathered here
to work for a greater togetherness and harmony.
May we care for one another
and the health and well-being
of every member of our community.
We ask this through Christ our Lord.
Amen.

HYMN   Bind us together, Lord (HON/Source)

ALTERNATIVES

READING   See Additional readings, number 24 (page 127)

PRAYER   Lord, make me an instrument of your peace;
where there is hatred, let me sow love;
where there is injury, pardon;
where there is discord, union;
where there is doubt, faith;
where there is despair, hope;
where there is darkness, light;
where there is sadness, joy.
Attributed to St Francis of Assisi

A2 Need for one another

HYMN When I needed a neighbour (HON)

COMMENT The need we have for one another is a spiritual need; we need the warmth of friendship, the moral support of encouragement, the spirit of acceptance and love. Only the Spirit of God, working among us all the time, can give us that in a lasting and satisfying way.

READING No man is an island, entire of itself; every man is a piece of the continent, a part of the main. If a clod be washed away by the sea, Europe is the less, as well as if a promontory were, as well as if a manor of thy friend's or of thine own were. Any man's death diminishes me because I am involved in mankind, and therefore never send to know for whom the bell tolls; it tolls for thee.
John Donne

COMMENT That reading was from a famous English writer, John Donne. The important and famous words to remember were 'No man is an island'. We are not cut off from one another, like a tiny island way out in the Pacific Ocean; we need and depend on one another.

SCRIPTURE READING Romans 12:3-13 – preferably the following version from *New World*:

We who are the friends of Jesus are, as I have already said, like a human body with its different parts. We are many persons, but we are one 'body'. Each of us is like a different part of the body, and we are here to help one another, as the different parts of the body help one another.

Each of us has different gifts; God has seen to that. We must use them. For example: some of us are able to understand God's Way more clearly than others; some of us deal with business better; some of us are teachers; some of us are speakers. Let us use our different gifts with God's help. And so with everything we do. If we give, let us be generous givers; if we are leaders, let us be energetic leaders; if we are helping others, let us be cheerful helpers.

PRAYER Break through, break through, Lord God,
break through our meanness and narrow selfishness.
Make us care about every member of our forms and classes,
make us concerned about the lonely in our school,
make us realise the need we have for one another.

Open our eyes to our own selfishness,
that we may learn that we need others
as they need us.
Give us patience,
give us reconciliation,
for your name's sake.
Amen.

HYMN   A new commandment (HON/Source)

ALTERNATIVES

READING   See assembly A1

HYMNS   Bind us together, Lord (HON/Source)
Love is his word (HON)

PRAYERS   See assembly A1 or D31

A3 Communication

HYMN   Love is his word (HON)

READING 1   One word, it just takes one word,
to change your life for ever.
One sound uttered by breath,
lips and tongue can seal your fate,
for good or for ill.

Someone asks, 'Will you marry me?'
Your reply – 'Yes' or 'No' –
will for ever change your life –
especially if you say, 'Yes'.
Paul Frost

COMMENT   The written word is powerful, but equally powerful is the spoken word, especially if it commits you and changes your life. Jesus said, 'It is from the overflow of the heart that the mouth speaks.' In other words, the sort of people we are will show up in what we say and how we say it.

READING 2   She said, 'Yes', and she died instantly, with a bullet in her head. It was an ordinary school day at Columbine High School. No one suspected that by the end of the day thirteen students would be dead and many wounded. Cassie Bernall, a pretty 17-year-old, was in the library doing some school work. She did not know that it was Hitler's birthday and two black-clad fellow students planned to celebrate evil and find lasting fame – by killing and dying in his name. They pointed an automatic rifle at Cassie's head and asked, 'Do you believe in God?' Knowing her fate, but without hesitation, Cassie said, 'Yes', and she died. The youth of America now hail her as a martyr, because she could have said, 'No'.
Paul Frost

PRAYER   Father, words are powerful things.
They can make people happy or sad;
show bravery or cowardice.
Take control of me all through today.
Help me to control my tongue,
that I may speak
no angry word,
no cruel word,
no untrue word,
no ugly word.
Control my thoughts,

so that I may think
no impure thoughts,
no bitter, envious, or jealous thoughts,
no selfish thoughts.
Control my actions,
so that all through today
my work may be my best;
I may never be too busy to lend a hand
to those who need it;
I may do nothing
of which afterwards I would be ashamed.
All this I ask for Jesus' sake.
Amen.

HYMN Make me a channel of your peace (HON/Source)

ALTERNATIVES

HYMNS God is love (HON)
Lord, the light of your love (Shine, Jesus, shine) (HON/Source)

PRAYERS See assembly E44 or C21

READING See Additional readings, number 22 (see page 127)

A4 Truth

HYMN   Spirit of the living God (HON/Source)

COMMENT   One of the things we learn about life, as time passes, is that 'truth will out'. Truth seems to march on and manage to survive even when covered by lies.

READING   What kind of liar are you?
People lie because they don't remember clearly what they saw.
People lie because they can't help making a story better than it was the way it happened.
People tell 'white lies' so as to be decent to others.
People lie in a pinch, hating to do it, but lying on because it might be worse.
And people lie just to be liars for a crooked personal gain.
What sort of liar are you?
Which of these liars are you?
Carl Sandburg

COMMENT   It is an insult to call someone a liar, but, as the reading points out, most of us are guilty of telling untruths – for one reason or another – from time to time. But we should try always to be truthful; on truth trust is built. The Bible teaches the importance of truth.

SCRIPTURE READINGS   **A** 'Sanctify them in the truth; your word is truth.'
(5 READERS)   **B** 'When the Spirit of truth comes, he will guide you into the truth.'
C 'For this I was born and for this I have come into the world, to bear witness to the truth.'
D 'Everyone who is of the truth hears my voice.'
E 'You will know the truth, and the truth will make you free.'

PRAYER   O God,
you can see my inmost thoughts
and know me better than I know myself.
You understand the impulses I feel,
the ambitions I have,
the silent loneliness I experience.
Forgive me my sins against truth –
the untruth within me, the half-truths,
the evasions, the exaggerations,
the trying silences that deceive,
the masks I wear before the world.
Help me to see myself as I really am,
fill me with the courage I will need
if I am to seek the truth and live in truth.
Amen.

HYMN   Father, I place into your hands (last two verses) (HON)

ALTERNATIVES

HYMNS   He who would valiant be (HON)
Be thou my vision (HON/Source)

PRAYER   See assembly A3

Jan 2002

A5 Personal responsibility

HYMN   Give me joy in my heart (HON)

READING   The story is told of a king who placed a heavy stone in the middle of the road and then hid and watched to see who would remove it. Men of various classes came and worked their way round it, some loudly blaming the king for not keeping the highways clear, but all dodging the duty of getting it out of the way. At last a poor peasant, on his way to town with his burden of vegetables for sale, came, and, contemplating the stone, laid down his load and rolled the stone into the gutter. Then, turning round, he spied a purse that had lain right under the stone. He opened it and found it full of gold pieces with a note from the king saying it was for the one who removed the stone.

COMMENT   The poor peasant was rewarded because he took responsibility for what was wrong. If a chair falls over in class, do you pick it up or walk round it ? If an accident occurs or you do wrong, do you own up or say, 'It's not my fault'?

SCRIPTURE READING   Matthew 25:14-30 (or *New World*, page 84)

COMMENT   Reward was given according to the responsibility that each accepted.

PRAYER   Give me, O Lord, a sense of responsibility.
Give me a sense of responsibility to myself,
so that I may not waste the gifts
which you have given to me;
a sense of responsibility to my parents,
so that I may repay them
for all the love and care they have given to me;
a sense of responsibility to my school,
so that all the patient teaching I have received
will not be wasted;
a sense of responsibility to my friends,
so that I may not fail their trust in me.
Give me, O Lord, a sense of responsibility,
that I may grow to real maturity.
This I ask through Christ your Son.
Amen.

HYMN   God's Spirit is in my heart (HON)

ALTERNATIVES

HYMNS   The Spirit lives to set us free (HON)
Lord of all hopefulness (HON)

PRAYERS   See assembly E38 or B15

A6 Respect for self

HYMN   It's me, it's me, it's me, O Lord (HON)

READING 1   I understand more and more how true Daddy's words were when he said, 'All children must look after their own upbringing'. Parents can only give good advice or put them on the right paths, but the final forming of a person's character lies in his own hands.
Diary of Anne Frank

COMMENT   How are you looking after yourself? Anne Frank says, 'The final forming of a person's character lies in his own hands.' Today that forming will continue. What sort of a person are you forming yourself into? Are you, for example, always complaining, or are you grateful for what you have?

READING 2   Today upon a bus, I saw a lovely girl
with golden hair;
I envied her – she seemed so happy – and
wished I were as fair.
When suddenly she rose to leave, I saw
her hobble down the aisle;
she had one foot and wore a crutch, but
as she passed, a smile.
Oh, God, forgive me when I whine;
I have two feet – the world is mine!

And then I stopped to buy some sweets.
The lad who sold them had
such charm, I talked with him – he said to me:
'It's nice to talk with folks like you.
You see,' he said, 'I'm blind.'
Oh, God, forgive me when I whine;
I have two eyes – the world is mine!

Then, walking down the street, I saw
a child with eyes of blue.
He stood and watched the others play;
it seemed he knew not what to do.
I stopped for a moment, then I said:
'Why don't you join the others, dear?'
He looked ahead without a word, and then
I knew he could not hear.
Oh, God, forgive me when I whine;
I have two ears – the world is mine.

With feet to take me where I'd go,
with eyes to see the sunset's glow,
with ears to hear what I would know,
oh, God, forgive me when I whine;
I'm blessed, indeed! The world is mine.
Anon

PRAYER Give me a good digestion, Lord,
and also something to digest;
give me a healthy body, Lord,
with sense to keep it at its best.

Give me a healthy mind, good Lord,
to keep the good and pure in sight,
which seeing sin is not appalled
but finds a way to set it right.

Give me a mind that is not bored,
that does not whimper, whine or sigh;
don't let me worry overmuch
about the fussy thing called I.

Give me a sense of humour, Lord,
give me the grace to see a joke,
to get some happiness from life
and pass it on to other folk.

HYMN Give me joy in my heart (HON)

ALTERNATIVES

HYMNS Peace, perfect peace (HON/Source)
O the love of my Lord (HON)

READING See Additional readings, number 17 (page 124)

PRAYERS See assembly B13 or E38

A7 Respect for others

HYMN Love is his word (HON)

READING Yes, the first woman I saw I myself picked up from the street. She had been half eaten by the rats and ants. I took her to the hospital but they could not do anything for her. They only took her in because I refused to move until they accepted her. From there I went to the municipality and I asked them to give me a place where I could bring these people because on the same day I had found other people dying in the streets. The health officer of the municipality took me to the temple, the Kali Temple, and showed me the dormashalah where the people used to rest after they had done their worship of Kali goddess. It was an empty building; he asked me if I would accept it. I was very happy to have that place for many reasons, but especially knowing that it was a centre of worship and devotion of the Hindus. Within 24 hours we had our patients there and we started the work of the home for the sick and dying who are destitutes. Since then we have picked up over 23,000 people from the streets of Calcutta of which about 50 per cent have died.
Mother Teresa

COMMENT Many wonderful people over the centuries have put Jesus' words into practice. Mother Teresa is one of those who has done much for others.

SCRIPTURE READING John 13:33-35 (or *New World*, page 397)

PRAYER *Litany of caring*

READER Break down, O Lord, the wall of selfishness
that cuts us off from the needs of other people.
We could help them if we cared:

ALL Teach us, O God, to care.

READER The unpopular pupils whom we do not want to know,
because we are afraid of becoming unpopular ourselves.
We could help them if we cared:

ALL Teach us, O God, to care.

READER The dull, boring people, who are not actively disliked
but simply ignored, and therefore lonely.
We could help them if we cared:

ALL Teach us, O God, to care.

READER   All those who serve us each day
and whom we don't bother to treat with much courtesy,
but who may be hurt by our offhandedness.
We could help them if we cared:

ALL   Teach us, O God, to care.

READER   The old people who long for somebody young to talk to,
but whom we prefer not to bother about
because we find them tedious.
We could help them if we cared:

ALL   Teach us, O God, to care.

READER   All these and many others,
we have the power and opportunity to help, Lord.
Your Son would have used our opportunities:
teach us to use them willingly in his name.
Amen.

HYMN   A new commandment (HON / Source)

ALTERNATIVES

READING   See Additional readings, number 17 (page 124)

PRAYERS   Make us ever eager, Lord,
to share the good things that we have.
Grant us such a measure of your Spirit
that we may find more joy in giving than in getting.
Make us ready to give cheerfully without grudging,
secretly without praise,
and in sincerity without looking for gratitude,
for Jesus Christ's sake.
Amen.
John Hunter

See also assembly B16

A8 Judging others

HYMN   All people that on earth do dwell (HON/Source)

COMMENT   We sang '*All* people that on earth do dwell', which of course includes those we don't get on with, and those we look down on and make judgements about, because of their colour, age, or beliefs.

READING 1   The six-man crew were all regulars. Friends of many trips. The Corporation cart made its way along the street. Past the morning newspaper offices. Every few feet picking up the waste of an affluent society. The driver pulled away from the kerb and looked in his mirror as he passed a badly parked van. Then back along the kerb again. The driver raised the back of his truck to bring the rubbish forward, and the children loved it. The time in that narrow Belfast street was three minutes to twelve on Monday, 20 March 1972. Somewhere in a badly parked van behind the dustcart a tiny spark jumped. A spark so small that the naked eye couldn't have seen it. And in less time than it takes to tell, the parked van exploded. Flames leapt from her metal bodywork, flames red, yellow, and lilac wrapped in deep grey smoke. From the Belfast Corporation dust-cart the bodies flew. People screamed. Pieces of human flesh littered the street. Some lay for ever still while others incredibly picked themselves up and staggered shocked away. Six people died in that instant of time in Donegal Street, Belfast, on Monday, 20 March 1972 at 11.57 am. Protestant and Roman Catholic, they died together as they have so often since in other outrages. Old and young; they all died together.
Robin Williamson

COMMENT   'All died together.' Catholics and Protestants; young and old. As Jimmy Savile says in his book *God'll Fix It*, this judging of other people is 'an abuse of the mind' and there is another way to go about it.

READING 2   On one occasion, in Stoke Mandeville Hospital, we had three people from Northern Ireland. They were in different wards. In one ward was a soldier who had been caught in gunfire and the bullet had chipped the top of his spine and rendered him paraplegic. In another ward we had a girl of 13 – a very pretty girl – who just happened to be standing on a street corner. She took a bullet through the throat and that rendered her paraplegic. In yet another ward, we had one of the militant bodies. He was actually doing the firing at the time. He was in a wheelchair. If anyone wanted to look at the futility of that particular course of action, they had only to look at those three people. Three lives completely ruined. After a while, when they all started to recover, they all trundled their wheelchairs down to the hospital canteen. The four of us used to talk, and had a lot to talk about. I wish you could have seen four of us talking together. And three of them suffering from the same thing. Yet, would you believe it, they were the best of friends. So I was right in the first place. There is another way of doing things. What had happened in their situation was a mental abuse and that put these people into wheelchairs. They have learned to live with their afflictions.

Jimmy Savile

PRAYER   Almighty God,
help us not to abuse our minds;
help us not to judge others by appearances.
Help us, Lord, to understand
that no matter what colour we are,
or what age, or what we believe,
we are all equally your sons and daughters.
May we never intentionally give hurt or offence to anyone,
and help us to realise
that if we are all your sons and daughters
that makes us brothers and sisters in your family.
We ask for your help through Christ our Lord.
Amen.

HYMN   Let there be love shared among us (HON/Source)

ALTERNATIVES

HYMN   Make me a channel of your peace (HON/Source)

PRAYER   See assembly A3

A9 Personal integrity

HYMN   Breathe on me, Breath of God (HON/Source)

COMMENT   It is important that we grow up to be people of integrity. But what is 'integrity'? It is being true to yourself. Having high ideals and trying to live up to them. St Paul helps us to understand what it is.

SCRIPTURE READING   2 Corinthians 6:6-8 (or *New World*, page 229)

COMMENT   A person who is trying to live sincerely understands that God sees and knows all that he or she does.

SCRIPTURE READING   Psalm 139:1-6 – preferably the following version from *Winding Quest*:

You have searched the depth of my being, O God,
you know all about me –
when I'm resting,
when I'm working.
You have probed my deepest intentions,
tracking out the road I take
and my camping grounds.
You know me through and through,
understanding better than I what I'm trying to say.
You have laid siege to me
behind me and before me;
you have put your hand on my shoulder –
I don't know why.
All this is beyond me,
out of my reach –
I can't grasp it.

PRAYER   O Lord and Master,
you know us better than we know ourselves.
Like an X-ray, your Holy Spirit can see through us
and search out our weaknesses and our fears.
Pour your love into our hearts
that we may become the sort of people you want us to be.
Amen.

HYMN   I, the Lord of sea and sky (Here I am, Lord) (HON/Source)

ALTERNATIVES

HYMNS   O the love of my Lord (HON)
Amazing grace (HON/Source)

PRAYERS   Through every minute of this day,
be with me, Lord!
Through every day of all this week,
be with me, Lord!
Through every week of all this year,
be with me, Lord!
Through all the years of all this life,
be with me, Lord!
So shall the days and weeks and years,
be threaded on a golden cord,
and all draw on with sweet accord
unto your fullness, Lord.
That so, when time is past,
by grace, I may at last
be with you, Lord.
John Oxenham

See also assembly A4

A10 Respect for property

HYMN   Morning has broken (HON)

COMMENT   God has given us a beautiful world to live in, but it is often cluttered up and spoilt by human beings. Listen now to a reading about an animal who made a mess!

READING 1   A great writer, called Sir Osbert Sitwell, tells the story of a man who once captured a very attractive little beaver. He decided to keep it as a pet and take it to his country home. To get there he had to pass through New York and decided to spend the night there at his flat. His wife received the unexpected visitor kindly and it was decided that the best place for the animal to spend the night was in the drawing room. They placed a wooden box lined with straw in the room so that the beaver could curl up in it. They then locked the door, and went to bed. When they entered the room next morning they found nothing there except the beaver and a dam! The animal had got out of its box and accidentally knocked over a small table on which was a vase of flowers. The spilt water on the floor had brought all the beaver's dam-building instincts into play. It had carefully sawn up the valuable chairs and tables and with the aid of cushions and books had made a wonderful dam.
Maurice Nassan

COMMENT   The beaver was only acting according to his nature; it was a natural instinct that led him to destroy the furniture. We are not mere animals with an instinct to destroy. Some boys and girls act as though they are – defacing walls and desks, damaging others' clothes, dropping litter. It is a war against the beauty of God's creation, a disrespect of our surroundings. What we do to other people's property should tell us a great deal about ourselves. We are shaping ourselves in the wrong way – we are damaging ourselves as we damage things.

READING 2   Life is like a jem* in a crown,
something more precious than the things around.
Something to care for, preserve
and keep safe.

Like a diamond is cut, so is life.
We cut our lives
but some of us cut it wrongly
so it breaks in pieces
and is scattered around
and is useless,
a precious thing gone to waste.
J. Becken

The spelling of the original is retained.

PRAYER Lord God, help me to respect myself.
I have only one life which I can only live once.
Life is precious.
I am precious in your sight.
Help me to remember that each person is unique and special.
Help me, too, to respect your creation
and the things of nature. *Help me to respect the dignity of*
Help me to respect other people's property. *others by being very*
for you have told us that whatever we do to other people *mindful*
we do to you. *of what*
Amen. *I say about*
others.

HYMN Be still, for the presence of the Lord (HON/Source)

ALTERNATIVES

HYMNS All the nations (HON)
All things bright and beautiful (HON/Source)

PRAYERS See assembly G54 or E38 (alternative prayer)

CHRISTIAN FESTIVALS

B 11   Christmas – Incarnation

HYMN Majesty, worship his majesty (HON/Source)

READING 1 A man who fell 170 feet down an abandoned tin mine in Cornwall survived for five days, drinking rainwater which collected at the bottom of the shaft. He was rescued late last night and walked away into the night, cheerful and apparently unscathed. Firemen, police and coastguards who took part in the rescue were surprised that 50-year-old John Elmes, a Londoner without a settled home, was found. The shaft is at Kenidjack, an area near St Just, close to Land's End, which is honeycombed with disused mines. It is shunned by local people. Three boys collecting firewood for a camp fire threw a stone down the shaft and heard Mr Elmes calling. He was brought to the surface strapped to a fireman who had been lowered down the mine. He believes that the shaft was on a slight slope and that he bounced from side to side as he tumbled to the bottom.
Anon

COMMENT Five days in darkness . . . in fear of your life ! Mankind was cut off from God, rather like that, before Jesus came as the Light of the World.

READING 2 *The Light of the World* is the title of a famous picture by Holman Hunt painted in 1854. It portrays Christ, thorn-crowned, and carrying a lantern, knocking at a closed door. When the artist showed the completed picture to some friends, one pointed out what seemed to be an omission. 'You have put no handle on the door,' he said to Holman Hunt. The artist replied, 'We must open to the Light – the handle is on the inside.'
Anon.

PRAYER Lord God,
our need of you is greater than we know or understand;
do not wait, do not delay,
but come quickly to our aid.
As you come to us, Lord, bring us forgiveness;
we are ungrateful to those who love us;
we are indifferent to the needs of others;
where we see injustice we do not protest;
help us to love others with the love you have shown us.
Bring us peace
that we may meet difficulties and disappointments
with calm and courage.
Bring us joy, because God has become one of us
so that all human beings may be free of darkness,
free of fear,
as members of the family of God.
Amen.

HYMN The Virgin Mary had a baby boy (HON)

ALTERNATIVES

HYMNS From heaven you came, helpless babe (The Servant King) (HON/Source)
Lord Jesus Christ (HON)

READINGS See Additional readings, numbers 7 (page 121) and 17 (page 124)

PRAYERS See assembly B16, B15 or E35

B12 Christmas – The gift of love

HYMN   We three Kings of Orient are (HON)

COMMENT   'Bearing gifts', the Wise Men, or Magi, came to the stable where Jesus was born.

SCRIPTURE READING   Matthew 2:1-12

READING

Did you, Lord Jesus, play with toys
like other little girls and boys;
a lamb your mother made with care
from bits of wool she had to spare?
And did you gurgle with delight
and have it in your cot at night?

Did Joseph, of a winter's night,
sit whittling by the fire's light,
the day's work done, all else was dark,
and make for you a Noah's ark,
a sturdy ship of wood and glue,
and wooden creatures, two by two?

The Magi, seeking you from far,
who found you by the wandering star,
brought gifts, such costly gifts they were,
of gold and frankincense and myrrh;
then you did bless their will to please,
but could not play with gifts like these.

What, then, O Jesus, should I bring
in homage to my infant King?
The poorest present, so I'm told,
if given from the heart, is gold,
and fragrant as the frankincense
when love is not the least expense.

Then token be the gift I bear
of lasting loving like the myrrh.
Killian Twell

PRAYER

Eternal God,
we thank you for showing yourself to us in Jesus Christ;
help us now to prepare to celebrate his birth with joy.
We thank you for the birth, childhood
and manhood of Jesus;

may we find in each moment of his life
the revelation of your love for us.
We pray that Christ may become alive in each one of us,
so that through us his love may be visible to all.
We pray at this time for the world,
where love and justice struggle
against war and oppression,
wastefuless and extravagance.
May the love of the Lord Jesus draw us to himself;
may the power of the Lord Jesus
strengthen us in his service;
may the joy of the Lord Jesus fill our hearts.
Amen.

HYMN   The first Nowell (HON)

ALTERNATIVES

HYMN   As with gladness men of old (HON)

PRAYER   God, this is your world,
you made us,
you love us;
teach us how to live
in the world that you have made.
Hope Freeman

B13 Christmas –
The dignity of the individual

HYMN   In the bleak midwinter (HON)

COMMENT   The last verse of that carol is rather beautiful and full of meaning: 'What can I give him . . . yet what I can I give him – give my heart.' Our reading today is about a little boy that gave what was most dear to him.

READING   One Christmas, Santa Claus brought me a toy engine. I took it with me to the convent, and played with it while mother and the nuns discussed old times. But it was a young nun who brought us in to see the crib. When I saw the Holy Child in the manger I was distressed because, little as I had, he had nothing at all. For me it was fresh proof of the incompetence of Santa Claus. I asked the young nun politely if the Holy Child didn't like toys, and she replied composedly enough, 'Oh he does, but his mother is too poor to afford them.' That settled it. My mother was poor too, but at Christmas she at least managed to buy me something, even if it was only a box of crayons. I distinctly remember getting into the crib and putting the engine between his outstretched arms. I probably showed him how to wind it as well, because a small baby like that would not be clever enough to know. I remember too the tearful feeling of reckless generosity with which I left him there in the nightly darkness of the chapel, clutching my toy engine to his chest.
Frank O'Connor

COMMENT   Our dignity as persons rests more on what we *are* than on what we have.

PRAYER   I asked God for strength that I might achieve;
I was made weak that I might learn humbly to obey.

I asked for help that I might do greater things;
I was given infirmity that I might do better things.

I asked for riches that I might be happy;
I was given poverty that I might be wise.

I asked for all things that I might enjoy life;
I was given life that I might enjoy all things.

I was given nothing that I asked for;
but everything that I had hoped for.

Despite myself, my prayers were answered;
I am among all people the most richly blessed.
Anon

HYMN   Come, come, come to the manger (HON)

ALTERNATIVES

HYMNS   See, amid the winter's snow (HON)
The Virgin Mary had a baby boy (HON)

PRAYERS   See assembly B15 or B14

B14 Easter – Christ's sacrifice

HYMN Majesty, worship his majesty (HON/Source)

READING During a cruel and bloody war, a commander took an oath in the presence of his troops that he would slaughter the entire population of a certain town, and in due course the bloodhounds of war were let loose on the defenceless people.

Now it so happened that a fugitive, seeking for a shelter, saw a sight which was indirectly the means of saving both his own life and the lives of others. He spied a number of soldiers as they broke into a house, the inmates of which they put to the sword. On leaving it, they fastened up the place again, and one of them, dipping a cloth in a pool of blood, splashed it on the door, as a token to any who might follow of what had taken place inside. Quick as his feet could carry him, the poor fugitive sped away to a large house in the centre of the town where a number of his friends were concealed, and breathlessly told them what he had seen. At once it flashed upon them how to act. A goat was in the yard. It was immediately killed, and its blood splashed on the door. Scarcely could they close the door again when a band of soldiers rushed into the street and began to slay right and left. But when they came to the blood-marked door they made no attempt to enter. The sword – so they thought – had already entered and performed its work in that house. Thus, while the many around were put to death, all inside the blood-sprinkled door were saved.
Anon

COMMENT The blood sprinkled on the door saved the people hiding in the house, in the same way that the angel of death passed over the houses where the Hebrews had marked their doorposts with blood.

SCRIPTURE READING Exodus 12:21-27 (or *Winding Quest*, page 103)

COMMENT It was the very night when Jesus and his friends were celebrating the Passover – the anniversary of the night when Moses and the Hebrews had escaped slavery in Egypt – that Jesus went out to his death. The shedding of his blood saved us from death.

HYMN From heaven you came (The Servant King) (HON/Source)

PRAYER Thanks be to you, Lord Jesus Christ,
for all the good things that you have given us;
for all the pains and insults which you accept for us.
O most merciful redeemer, friend and brother,
may we know you more clearly, love you more dearly
and follow you more nearly, day by day.
St Richard of Chichester

ALTERNATIVES

HYMNS   Were you there (HON)
Amazing grace (HON/Source)

PRAYERS   See assembly B16 or A1 (alternative prayer)

B15 Easter – Risen Lord

HYMN Morning has broken (HON)

COMMENT If you wake in the middle of the night, you know that no matter how dark it is, how still all around seems, how dead all living things appear, the morning will come and light will overcome darkness.

READING
At three o'clock in the morning
if you open your window and listen
you will hear the feet of the wind
that is going to call the sun,
and the trees in the darkness rustle,
and the trees in the moonlight glisten,
and though it is deep dark night,
you know that the night is done.
Anon

SCRIPTURE READING John 20:1-18 (or *New World*, page 407)

COMMENT Christ said, 'I am the Light of the World', and his rising from the dead is a victory for light over darkness, goodness over evil, life over death.

PRAYER
O You who are the light of the minds that know you,
the life of the souls that love you,
and the strength of the wills that serve you,
help us to know you better, that we may truly love you;
and so love you that we may fully serve you;
whom to love and serve is perfect freedom;
through Jesus Christ our Lord.
Gelasian Sacramentary

HYMN Now the green blade riseth (HON)

ALTERNATIVES

PRAYER See assembly E43

B16 Easter – Living Lord

HYMN   This is the day (HON)

READING   Elizabeth Pilenko was a well-educated Russian, brought up in a rich family owning land in the south of Russia. During the Revolution she supported those who were trying to obtain justice for the peasants. A few years later she settled in Paris and there became a Christian. She founded a convent and, as Mother Maria, she spent her life caring for the Russian refugees who fled to France to escape the violence of the revolutionaries.

In 1940 France became an occupied country. Mother Maria opened the doors of her convent as a haven for Jews persecuted by the German army of occupation. She knew the risks she was running. After a month of helping hundreds of Jews to escape to safety, the Gestapo arrived at the convent. Mother Maria was arrested and sent to the concentration camp at Ravensbruck. There she continued to give herself unceasingly for the suffering prisoners. Even the guards acknowledged her goodness, calling her 'that wonderful Russian nun'. After she had spent two and a half years in the camp a new block of buildings went up. The prisoners were told that they were hot baths. In fact, they were gas chambers where the mass execution of prisoners would take place.

One day a few dozen women prisoners were lined up by the guards outside the new buildings. One of the girls in the line became hysterical. Mother Maria was not one of those chosen to enter the buildings. She came up to the girl and said, 'Don't be frightened. Look, I shall take your turn.' In line with the rest, she passed through the door. It was Good Friday, 1945.
Frances Stantan

COMMENT   It is hardly likely that we will ever have the opportunity to give our lives for another person, but we do have the daily opportunity of living for others – helping others.

PRAYER   Christ has
no body on earth but yours,
no hands but yours,
no feet but yours.
Yours are the eyes
through which is to look out
Christ's compassion to the world.
Yours are the feet

with which he is to go about
doing good.
Yours are the hands
with which he is to bless people now.
Amen.

HYMN   Be still, for the presence of the Lord (HON)

ALTERNATIVES

HYMNS   From heaven you came (The Servant King) (HON/Source)
At the name of Jesus (HON/Source)

PRAYERS   See assembly D35 or B19

B17 Pentecost – Fire of the Spirit

HYMN   Spirit of the living God (HON / Source)

COMMENT   'Fire!' If someone rushed in here now calling, 'Fire, Fire!' we would put our fire drill into operation. If we didn't, lives might be at risk. Listen now to the words of a ballad by Fred Dallas about a terrible fire that raged for four days in 1958 in Smithfield Market, London.

READING   On the coldest day in all the year,
it was a Thursday morning,
and the hottest place in London
was the Smithfield Market burning.
It burned four days without a pause,
it melted all the snow;
and two brave men were choked to death,
trapped in the smoke below.
They died there down below.

It was down there underneath the ground
the fire it started burning,
it raged along each storage hall
and round each passage turning.
The melted fat flared in the fire
and filled the air with smoke.
The firemen they wore gas masks
for fear that they would choke,
down in the terrible smoke.

Ten minutes was the longest time
that they could stay down there,
for the heat and the fumes and the burning fat
was more than they could bear;
but two men lost their way below
and lay down there to die.
The searchers found them, but too late
to lead them to the sky.
They laid them 'neath the sky.

Another day had passed
when an explosion rocked the town.
The fire broke out into the air
and Smithfield towers came down.
One hundred feet into the air
and burning flames leapt high.
From Clerkenwell to London Bridge

we saw them in the sky.
They lit up all the sky.

From every London fire brigade,
they came to fight the flames.
A thousand firemen heroes
and we don't know all their names;
but two men died and two wives cried,
and three young children too.
Remember them and all the men
who fight the fires for you,
who die in the fires for you.
Fred Dallas

COMMENT Fire does not, of course, just kill and destroy. It can give light and comfort; it can warm, protect, and cleanse. It is not surprising that God used fire as a symbol of the presence of his Spirit.

SCRIPTURE READINGS
(3 READERS)

A There God appeared to Moses in the shape of a flame of fire, coming from the middle of a bush. *Exodus 3:2*
B Moses led the people of the camp to meet God; and they stood at the bottom of the mountain. The mountain of Sinai was entirely wrapped in smoke, because God had descended on it in the form of fire. *Exodus 19:18*
C When Pentecost day came round, they had all met in one room, when suddenly they heard what sounded like a powerful wind from heaven, the noise of which filled the entire house in which they were sitting, and something appeared to them that seemed like tongues of fire; these separated and came to rest on the head of each of them. *Acts 2:3*

PRAYER O God our Father,
we thank you for fire.
It warms us, comforts us and can provide light for us.
May the fire of your Holy Spirit warm our hearts,
comfort us when we are lonely and worried,
and light up our minds and hearts.
Amen.

HYMN Colours of day (HON/Source)

ALTERNATIVES

HYMN All over the world (HON/Source)

READING See Additional readings, number 3 (page 119)

PRAYER See assembly B15

B18 Pentecost – Symbol of wind

HYMN   The Spirit lives to set us free (HON)

READING   Rumbling in the chimneys, rattling at the doors,
round the roofs and round the roads the rude wind roars;
raging through the darkness, raving through the trees,
racing off again across the great grey seas.
Rodney Bennett

COMMENT   On a stormy night the wind can fill us with fear. Sometimes we
read or hear about hurricanes that tear up houses and toss cars and
people about. God has in the past used the symbol of wind for the
power of his presence.

SCRIPTURE READINGS   **A** Exodus 14:19-22 (or *Winding Quest*, page 106)
(2/3 READERS)   **B** 1 Kings 19:9-24 (or *Winding Quest*, page 22)

COMMENT   When God's Spirit came upon the first followers of Jesus at Pentecost
time, his approach was announced by the blowing of a strong wind.

SCRIPTURE READING   **C** Acts 2:1-11 (or *New World*, page 163)

PRAYER   May the strength of God pilot us.
May the power of God preserve us.
May the wisdom of God instruct us.
May the hand of God protect us.
May the way of God direct us.
May the shield of God defend us.
May the host of God guard us
against the snares of evil
and the temptations of the world.
St Patrick's Breastplate

HYMN   Spirit of the living God (HON/Source)

ALTERNATIVES

READING   See Additional readings, number 1 (page 119)

HYMN   God's Spirit is in my heart (HON)

PRAYERS   See assembly B15 or C25

B19 Pentecost – Breath of God

HYMN Breathe on me, Breath of God (HON/Source)

COMMENT The greatest thing that God ever did, and carries on doing, was to make the universe – all the stars and planets, seas and oceans, plants and animals. Finally he made something in his own image – human beings.

READING God created the world and set man in it
and he loved him.
Up from the bed of the river
God scooped the clay,
and by the bank of the river
he kneeled him down.
And there the great God almighty,
who lit the sun and fixed it in the sky,
who flung the stars to the most far corner of night,
who rounded the earth in the middle of his hand,
this great God,
like a mother bending over her baby,
kneeled down in the dust,
toiling over a lump of clay
till he shaped it in his own image.
There into it he blew the breath of life
and man became a living soul.
James Weldon Johnson

COMMENT Listen now to two short Bible readings. The first should help you to understand the second.

SCRIPTURE READINGS **A** Ezekiel 37:1-10
(2 READERS) **B** John 20:19-23

COMMENT It was because the Apostles were lifeless – full of fear and anxiety – that Jesus needed to breathe on them and fill them with his brave Spirit. After they had received the Holy Spirit the first thing they did was to go out into the streets to tell people the truth about Jesus.

PRAYER Lord, be with us this day.
Within us to purify us;
above us to draw us up;
beneath us to sustain us;
before us to lead us;
behind us to restrain us;
around us to protect us.
St Patrick

HYMN   Colours of day (HON/Source)

ALTERNATIVES

HYMN   I, the Lord of sea and sky (Here I am, Lord) (HON/Source)

PRAYERS   See assembly B15 or B13

B20 The Holy Trinity

HYMN Holy, holy, holy! Lord God almighty (HON/Source)

COMMENT Christian teaching about the Holy Trinity is among the most important but also the most difficult for us to grasp. Here are some words from Jimmy Savile about the Trinity.

READING I believe that people latch on to different parts of the God family to suit themselves. After all, all Christian beliefs that are formulated in this sort of way – like the Holy Trinity – are only the ways that men and women have of describing God.

When the Fathers of the Early Church wanted to find some words to describe God, they came up with the Holy Trinity. It's all a bit mathematical. That sort of formula might put people off. As far as I'm concerned, the Holy Trinity means that God is in one lump! It is just God's three ways of being God. I can't say I think a lot about the Holy Trinity or about God the Holy Spirit, because my religion is very much a practical religion, although I do have a great sense of history and tradition. If you feel more at home talking about God the Holy Spirit, then use that. After all, the Holy Spirit, I think, is just another way of talking about the spirit of Jesus.
Jimmy Savile

COMMENT Jimmy is not an expert on the Christian Faith and he's wrong about one thing. It may appear to be mathematical – but it isn't, nor is there any likelihood of the number of persons changing. It's more like God's intimate family life, where total love is the bond and uniting force between the persons of the Trinity. God is one, and he has told us, 'God is all love'. Love unites and total love unites totally.

SCRIPTURE READINGS
(4 READERS)

A Do you not believe that I am in the Father and the Father is in me? *John 14:10*

B If anyone loves me he will keep my word, and my Father will love him, and we shall come to him and make our home with him. *John 14:23*

C Anyone who fails to love can never have known God, because God is love. *1 John 4:8*

D No one has ever seen God; but as long as we love one another God will live in us and his love will be complete in us. We can know that we are living in him and he is living in us because he lets us share his Spirit. *1 John 4:12-13*

PRAYER   All our prayers, Almighty Father,
are offered to you through your Son Jesus Christ.
Fill us with your Holy Spirit,
so that with a deeper love and trust in you
we may build up our Christian life
with more frequent prayer.
This we ask, in the Holy Spirit
and through Jesus, your Son.
Amen.

HYMN   Love is his word (HON)

ALTERNATIVES

HYMN   God's Spirit is in my heart (HON)

PRAYER   I bind unto myself today
the Power of God to hold and lead,
his eye to watch, his might to stay,
his ear to harken to my need;
the wisdom of my God to teach,
his hand to guide, his shield to ward;
the word of God to give me speech,
his heavenly host to be my guard.
St Patrick

CHRISTIAN CALLING AND LIFE

C21 Christian vocation

HYMN I, the Lord of sea and sky (Here I am, Lord) (HON/Source)

SCRIPTURE READING 1 Samuel 3:3-11

COMMENT That reading was about a call from God which we find in the Old Testament. In the Gospels we find Jesus calling men and women to follow him. Some respond and do follow him – and some do not.

SCRIPTURE READINGS **A** Matthew 9:9
(3 READERS) **B** Matthew 4:18-19
C Matthew 19:16-22

COMMENT The Apostles left their jobs and followed Jesus. The rich young man was called too, but there was an obstacle in the way which prevented him joining Jesus. He could not leave his rich and comfortable way of life. Jesus calls us. What do we put in the way of following him more faithfully?

PRAYER Dear Lord Jesus, teach us to be generous,
to serve you as you deserve,
to give and not to count the cost,
to fight and not to heed the wounds,
to toil and not to seek for rest,
to labour and ask for no reward
save that of knowing that we do your will.
Amen.
St Ignatius Loyola

HYMN Follow me, follow me (HON)

ALTERNATIVES

HYMN   Lord, the light of your love (Shine, Jesus, shine) (HON/Source)

PRAYER   O Lord Jesus Christ,
who are the way, the truth and the life,
we pray,
do not suffer us to stray from you, who are the way,
nor to distrust you, who are the truth,
nor to rest on any other than you, who are the life.
Teach us what to believe, what to do
and wherein to take our rest.
Amen.
Erasmus

C22 Baptism

HYMN Do not be afraid (HON)

READING 1 St Louis of France used to sign his documents not 'Louis IX, King' but 'Louis of Poissy'. Someone asked him why, and he answered, 'Poissy is the place where I was baptised. I think more of the place where I was baptised than of Rheims Cathedral where I was crowned. It is a greater thing to be a child of God than to be the ruler of a kingdom: this last I shall lose at death, but the other will be my passport to an everlasting glory.'
Anon

COMMENT King Louis knew where he was baptised. Do you know where and when you became a child of God? Do you realise the importance of that day?

READING 2 When the Roman youth reached manhood, he put on the *toga virilis,* the robe of manhood. The day was one of special ceremonial, a great day for him.

When the Hindu youths of certain castes reach manhood, they put on the *Yagnopavitam* or sacred cord. The day is one of special ceremonial, a great day for the youth who is invested with the sacred cord.

So the believer at his baptism acknowledges that he has 'put on Christ' – a new robe of righteousness to display to the world, a new cord of holiness that links him with the holiness of his God, a 'Holy Father'.
Anon

PRAYER Almighty Father,
at my baptism I became a child of God – your child.
You adopted me into your family, the family of God.
Help me to understand the importance
of that wonderful event;
help me to live up to the dignity expected of a child of God;
help me to avoid anything that might bring disgrace
to the name 'Christian'.
Please give me this help through Christ your Son.
Amen.

HYMN Father, I place into your hands (HON/Source)

ALTERNATIVES

HYMN   The Lord's my shepherd (HON/Source)

READING   See Additional readings, number 24 (page 127)

PRAYERS   See assembly C25 or C21 (alternative prayer)

C23 Eucharist

HYMN   Love is his word (HON)

COMMENT   In the name of love, people will dare to do anything, willingly placing their lives at risk.

READING   Stories continue to come out of China, from time to time, of the heroic efforts of the few remaining bishops and priests to keep the faith alive and nourish the underground Church. One such story tells of a priest who lives and works as a coolie. By means of pre-arranged sign language he gets messages around of where he is to be found – usually in the corner of a local market, selling soap. Customers who, like the early Christians, give a secret sign, are given a special piece of soap, between the wrappings of which is hidden a small wafer of consecrated bread. The Chinese Christian takes his purchase home and usually after a short family service receives Communion.
Anon

COMMENT   Why, throughout the centuries, have men and women risked imprisonment, torture and death to receive such a small thing – a consecrated piece of bread?

SCRIPTURE READING   1 Corinthians 11:23-25

COMMENT   To do what Christ did, to share what he shared, at his last meal with his friends, is for Christians an expression of their love for their Saviour.

PRAYER   Almighty Father,
love is expressed in giving
and your Son showed you perfect love
by giving himself to you, in perfect obedience.
Out of love he offers himself to us too,
in Holy Communion.
May we take every opportunity
of accepting the gift he offers us,
and may we grow in your love
to become more and more like Jesus Christ your Son.
This we ask through him.
Amen.

HYMN   Be still, for the presence of the Lord (HON/Source)

ALTERNATIVES

HYMN   This is my body (HON)

PRAYERS   O Lord our God,
grant us grace to desire you with our whole heart,
so that desiring you we may seek and find you;
and so finding you, may love you;
and loving you, may hate those sins
which separate us from you,
for the sake of Jesus Christ.
Amen.
St Anselm

See also assembly B14

C24 Faith

HYMN   I, the Lord of sea and sky (HON/Source)

READING   One of the stories told of a persecution in China in the old days is about a Chinese Christian lad named Paul Moy. He was dragged before the local mandarin, who tried to induce him to renounce the Christian faith. Other persuasions having failed, the mandarin tried bribery, and promised the boy a purse of silver. 'I thank your Excellency, but a purse of silver is not enough.' 'Very well: I will give you a purse of gold.' 'Excellency, that is still not enough.'

The magistrate had not expected such obstinate bargaining on the part of one so young and was rather annoyed. 'Well, what do you want, then?' 'Most noble Excellency, if you ask me to renounce the Faith you will have to give me enough to buy a new soul.' The magistrate was not amused! Paul completed his glorious witness when he was beheaded a few days later.
Anon

COMMENT   Such courage needs not just faith in the sense of a strong belief, but faith in the sense of tremendous trust in God's loving care of us.

LET US PRAY

PRAYER   Lord, give me faith! – to live from day to day;
with tranquil heart to do my simple part,
and, with my hand in yours, just go your way.

Lord, give me faith! – to trust, if not to know;
with quiet mind in all things you to find,
and, child-like, go where you would have me go.

Lord, give me faith! – to leave it all to you;
the future is your gift, I would not lift
the veil your love has hung between it and me.
John Oxenham

HYMN   Lord of all hopefulness (HON)

ALTERNATIVES

HYMNS   Firmly I believe and truly (HON)
Immortal, invisible, God only wise (HON/Source)

PRAYER   See assembly B13

C25 Mission

HYMN God's Spirit is in my heart (HON)

SCRIPTURE READING Luke 4:16-22 (or *New World*, page 134)

COMMENT Jesus had a mission in life to accomplish; we have just heard how he first announced that mission. He called others to help him.

SCRIPTURE READING Matthew 10:1-10 (or *New World*, page 12)

COMMENT The friends Jesus sent out to continue his work had to face much hardship. This, for example, is what Paul had to suffer.

SCRIPTURE READING 2 Corinthians 11:23-28 (or *New World*, page 222)

PRAYER Go forth into the world in peace,
be of good courage;
hold fast that which is good;
render to no man evil for evil;
strengthen the faint-hearted;
support the weak;
help the afflicted;
honour all men;
love and serve the Lord,
rejoicing in the power of the Holy Spirit.
And the blessing of God almighty,
the Father, the Son and the Holy Spirit
be upon us and remain with us for ever.
Amen.
From an alternative order of Confirmation in the Prayer Book as proposed in 1928

HYMN Lord, the light of your love (Shine, Jesus, shine) (HON/Source)

ALTERNATIVES

HYMN Colours of day (HON/Source)

PRAYER See assembly A1 (alternative prayer)

OUR RELATIONSHIP WITH GOD

D26 Trust in God

HYMN O Lord, my God (HON/Source)

COMMENT One of the mysteries of God is how he is infinite, all mighty and perfect in every way, but at the same time very close to us, wanting us to trust in him.

READING Bruce Larson tells a story in his book *Edge of Adventure.* It's about a letter found in a baking-powder tin wired to the handle of an old pump which offered the only hope of drinking water on a very long and seldom-used trail across the Amargosa Desert, in the USA; the letter read as follows:

This pump is all right as of June 1932. I put the new leather sucker washer into it, and it ought to last several years. But this leather washer dries out and the pump has got to be primed. Under the white rock, I buried a bottle of water. There's enough water in it to prime the pump, but not if you drink some first. Pour in about one-quarter, and let her to wet the leather. Then pour in the rest, medium fast, and pump like crazy. You'll get water. The well has never run dry. Have faith. When you get watered up, fill the bottle and put it back like you found it for the next feller.
(signed) Desert Pete.

PS. Don't go drinking up the water first. Prime the pump with it first, and you'll get all you can hold.

COMMENT Desert Pete asks for trust in a dangerous situation. If we trust God in the same way and leave ourselves and everything that worries us in the hands of our loving Father, that confidence will always be rewarded.

PRAYER   Father,
I place myself lovingly, confidently in your hands.
Do with me what you will.
You have made me,
you know me better than I know myself –
what have I to fear, if I place all my trust in you?
Please hear my prayer through Christ your Son.
Amen.

HYMN   Do not be afraid (HON)

ALTERNATIVES

HYMNS   Lead us, heavenly Father, lead us (HON/Source)
Lord of all hopefulness (HON)

PRAYER   See assembly C24

D27 Conscience

HYMN   Give me joy in my heart (HON)

COMMENT   There will be joy in our hearts if we have clear consciences. There will be peace in our hearts if our consciences are at ease, because we are trying to love in the right way. That means not turning our love in on ourselves but out towards others.

READING   King Oswin was troubled to think of Bishop Aidan's long journeys on foot on the rough roads and among the stony crags of Yorkshire, and he knew that the Bishop must often find it difficult to cross the rivers, for there were few bridges. So he gave him a fine horse with royal trappings, to help him on his journeys. One day as Aidan was riding the horse over the moorlands he met a beggar who asked for alms. At once he dismounted and gave the horse to the poor man, and went on his way on foot. This was told to the king, who felt rather hurt that Aidan should have given away the horse he had particularly chosen for him as a gift. As they were going in to dinner he said to him, 'Have I not many less valuable horses which might have been given to the beggar?' And Aidan, who was ever a friend of the poor, replied with his ready wit, 'What sayest thou, King? Is that son of a mare more precious in thy sight than the son of God?'

They went into the hall, and Aidan took his place at the table, but the king, who had been out hunting, stood warming himself at the fire with his attendants. Suddenly he ungirded his sword and threw himself at Aidan's feet, asking his forgiveness. 'I will never speak any more of this,' he said, 'nor will I ever judge what, or how much, you shall give to the sons of God.'
Phyllis Garlick

COMMENT   Even a great king can and must respond to his conscience. We must always listen and be guided by it.

PRAYER   O You, who are the light of the minds that know you;
the life of the souls that love you;
and the strength of the wills that serve you;
help us so to know you that we may truly love you;
so to love you that we may fully serve you;
whom to serve is perfect freedom;
through Jesus Christ our Lord.
Amen.
Gelasian Sacramentary

HYMN   The King of love my shepherd is (HON)

ALTERNATIVES

HYMN   All you who seek a comfort sure (HON)

PRAYERS   See assembly G60 or C23 (alternative prayer)

D28 Courage

HYMN   I, the Lord of sea and sky (HON)

READING 1   In one of the terrible concentration camps of the Second World War there was a Polish priest, called Father Kolbe. He had been put there because he had published comments about the Nazi regime. One of the prisoners escaped from the camp and the camp commandant, to punish the prisoners, ordered ten of them to be starved to death. Among the prisoners was a young man who had a wife and children. When the prisoners' numbers were called out, Father Kolbe stepped forward and insisted on taking the young man's place. In the death cell Father Kolbe helped the others prepare for death; he was the last to die. Because he had taken too long they injected poison into his arm. After his death, if you had gone into his cell, you would have seen a picture of Jesus on the cross scratched on the wall with his nails.
Anon

COMMENT   Courage like that of Father Maximilian Kolbe, now St Maximilian Kolbe, is so heroic and extraordinary. We are not likely ever to be called upon to be so brave, but quite often we all have to show courage in small things. Jesus showed us how to be brave.

SCRIPTURE READING   John 18:1-12 (or *New World*, page 400)

PRAYER   Lord Jesus, in the garden
you were faced with the fear of suffering and death.
You did what you have told us to do
when faced with fear and suffering.
You prayed.
You were supported by your Father's love,
wanting only to do what he asked of you.
Your trust and confidence in God was rewarded.
You rose from the dead, our Saviour and Lord.
Now you support us when we are anxious and afraid.
Give us courage in both the big and small things of life;
help us always to seek to do your will.
Amen.

HYMN   Do not be afraid (HON)

ALTERNATIVES

HYMN   Father, I place into your hands (HON/Source)

PRAYERS   See assembly B14 or A3

D29 Confidence in God

HYMN   Father, I place into your hands (HON/Source)

SCRIPTURE READING   Mark 4:35-41 (or *New World*, page 13)

COMMENT   This is the only time – with the exception of the end of Jesus' life, when the friends of Jesus were so frightened that they ran away – when we hear that they were afraid. The storm must have been very violent and terrifying for experienced fishermen to have feared for their lives.

SCRIPTURE READING   Matthew 6:23-24 (or *New World*, page 97)

PRAYER   Lord Jesus, I have watched the sea
when I have been to the coast on holiday.
Even in summer, the waves pound the beach
and hiss over the shingle as if they were living, angry things.

I have watched the sea on the television news in winter
when great breakers have pounded the promenades
and tossed cars about as if with a giant hand.

I'm always a bit afraid of the sea, Lord,
even in its summer moods.

Yet you could stand erect in a heaving boat
and command the tumbling waves to be still.
No wonder your disciples were amazed.
What courage you showed!

Please share that courage with me, Lord Jesus.
Great waves of temptation bear against the shores of my heart.
Help me to still the storm,
and bring me to the safe harbour of your peace.
Mary Drewery

HYMN   Peace is flowing like a river (HON)

ALTERNATIVES

HYMNS   Do not be afraid (HON)
Lead us, heavenly Father, lead us (HON/Source)

PRAYERS   See assembly A1 (alternative prayer) or A9 (alternative prayer)

D30 No trust in riches

HYMN	He's got the whole world in his hand (HON)
COMMENT	Today we have two readings about people who put money first in their lives.
READING 1	A miser in France used to keep all his gold and precious things in a cellar under the floor of his house. One day he went down through a secret trap-door at the top of the cellar to gloat over his treasure. Then the trap-door banged down so that he could not get out. No one in the house knew about the cellar and the miser could not be found. People searched all over the place without finding him. After a long time they gave up and the house was sold. The new people who bought the house wanted some new building work done and the cellar was discovered. When it was opened the miser was found sitting at the table with all his gold glittering around him. The dead man had even eaten a candle before dying of hunger. *Maurice Nassan*
READING 2	One summer afternoon a boat, crowded with passengers, many of them miners from California, suddenly struck a submerged wreck as it sped down the Mississippi. In a moment her deck was a wild confusion. The boats were able to take off only one-fourth of the passengers: the rest, throwing off many of their clothes, succeeded in swimming to shore. Immediately after the last had quit the vessel, a man appeared on deck. Seizing a spar, he leapt into the river but instantly sank like a stone. When his body was recovered, it was found that, while the other passengers were escaping, he had been rifling the miners' trunks, and round his waist he had fastened bags of gold. In a quarter of an hour he had amassed more than most men do in a lifetime; but he lost his life in an instant. *Anon*
COMMENT	Jesus had something to say about people who put their trust in money and not in him.
SCRIPTURE READINGS (3 READERS)	Jesus said: A 'How hard it is for those who have riches to enter the kingdom of God.' *Mark 10:23* B 'It is easier for a camel to pass through the eye of a needle than for a rich man to enter the kingdom of God.' *Mark 10:26* C 'Do not store up treasures for yourselves on earth, where moths and woodworms destroy them and thieves can break in and steal. But store up treasures for yourselves in heaven.' *Matthew 6:19-20*

COMMENT   As Christians our trust should not be in money and material things but in our God and his loving care of us. If we place ourselves trustingly in the hands of God, who has made us, our hearts will be light and joyful.

PRAYER   Generous and loving Father,
we have received so much from your hands.
We are rich in having enough food, water,
shelter, education and health care,
when many people in the world
do not have sufficient of these.
Help us not to be greedy, grasping after more.
Help us not to put possessions and things
before having care and love for others.
Help us to remember your warning
that it is difficult for the rich,
who place all their trust in money and possessions,
to come to you and be one with you.
Amen.

HYMN   Give me joy in my heart (HON)

ALTERNATIVES

HYMN   Be still and know that I am God (HON/Source)

READING   See Additional readings, number 4 (page 120)

PRAYERS   See assembly A13 or E40 (alternative prayer)

D31 Vocation

HYMN It's me, it's me, it's me, O Lord (HON)

COMMENT Everyone needs someone to talk to when they have a problem or feel lonely or depressed. In every town and city the Samaritans can be found; they are always ready to listen. This is the story of how they started.

READING Chad Varah was an Anglican priest. In 1953 he buried a girl of 18 who had killed herself. The coroner, at her inquest, suggested that she might not have done this desperate act if someone had been around who would have listened to her troubles. Chad Varah decided to use his London church and a telephone to listen to people who were in despair. He put a small advertisement in the local paper, and during the first week he had 27 calls.

Soon he was listening and advising people 12 hours each day. There were so many people waiting in his outer office to see him that he asked some of his congregation to come and provide cups of tea for them. Then he found that often people who had come into the outer office in great distress had become different people by the time they reached him, and some did not even wait to see him because one of the helpers had befriended them. So he decided to train a group of his congregation so that they could be more helpful in the way they befriended the clients.

That is how the Samaritans were formed.
Patricia Curley

COMMENT If Chad Varah had not gone to the inquest on the girl who had killed herself and heard the words of the coroner, he might never have started that wonderful organisation which has saved so many lives – the Samaritans. God spoke to him through that coroner. He was called to a special work.

SCRIPTURE READING Luke 10:1-12 (or *New World*, page 140)

COMMENT Jesus 'called' his friends to join him in his special work and sent them out to preach the Good News.

PRAYER O Divine Master, grant that I may seek not so much
to be consoled, as to console,
to be understood, as to understand,
to be loved, as to love;
for it is in giving that we receive,
it is in pardoning that we are pardoned,

and it is in dying that we are born to
eternal life.
Amen.
St Francis of Assisi

HYMN   From heaven you came (The Servant King) (HON/Source)

ALTERNATIVES

HYMN   All that I am (HON)

PRAYERS   See assembly C21 or A7 (alternative prayer)

D32 Respect for authority

HYMN	Majesty, worship is his majesty (HON/Source)
COMMENT	Christ, our King, commands our respect. All authority belongs to him. Respect for authority, which is the theme of this assembly, can be founded on fear or love.
READING	A new road was to be built and one day a government surveyor brought his theodolite along to a farm, called on the farmer and asked permission to set it up in a field nearby to take readings. Seeing the farmer's unwillingness to let him enter the field, the surveyor produced his warrant and explained that he had government authority for entering the field and could, on the same authority, go anywhere to take the necessary readings for the new road. Reluctantly the farmer opened the barred gate and allowed him to enter and set up his survey table, but went to the other end of the field and let in the fiercest of his bulls. The surveyor was greatly alarmed at seeing the bull approach, and the farmer from the other side of the gate shouted to him 'Show him your warrant card: show him your authority.' *Anon*
COMMENT	We can be obedient because we fear, or because we love and respect the person who asks for something of us.
SCRIPTURE READING	John 15:9-17 (or *New World*, page 396)
PRAYER	Lord, I know that the best way to respect your commandments is to think of them as coming from you as loving requests. One of the best ways I can show love for you is by loving other people. Sometimes this is easy – when I'm with people I like. Please help me when loving is hard, when people are unkind, when they don't understand – when I just don't like them. Teach me to love as you loved; help me to keep your commandments, for in that way I show love to you. Amen.
HYMN	Love is his word (HON)

ALTERNATIVES

HYMNS   Immortal, invisible, God only wise (HON/Source)
From heaven you came (The Servant King) (HON/Source)

PRAYERS   See assembly C25 or D31

D33 Forgiveness

HYMN   God forgave my sin (HON/Source)

READING 1   Rabbi Leo Baeck, a German scholar who took on the leadership of German Jews in Hitler's time, is a fine example of forgiveness. He was five times arrested, and finally sent to a concentration camp, where he served on the convicts' committee of management. On the very day he was to have been shot, the Russian troops arrived. Baeck could have escaped at once, but stayed behind to argue with the Russians, to persuade them to spare the lives of the German camp guards. The Russians decided that the camp guards should be handed over to the inmates. Baeck then argued with the inmates and managed to persuade them not to take the vengeance that they were thirsting for. Later on he went to the USA and worked hard for the Council of Christians and Jews. He died in 1956, aged 80.
Anon

READING 2   Suddenly Corrie caught sight of him in the congregation at Munich – the former SS man who had been their guard at Ravensbruck concentration camp. Somehow she managed to go on speaking, but the scenes of horror and anguish from those past days crowded into her mind. It was not for herself she cared – she remembered her poor sister, Betsie, ill, frail, yet made to strip while those mocking guards examined their helpless prisoners. Now the leader of them was here in church.

After the service he came up the church towards her, smiling broadly and with outstretched hand. 'Thank you for your message,' he said. 'Jesus has washed my sins away.' Corrie looked at him, unable to lift her hand from her side. She had preached forgiveness but now could she show it to the very person who had humiliated and hurt her beloved sister? For a long moment she paused, then prayed silently, 'Lord Jesus, forgive me and help me to forgive him.' But still she could neither smile nor raise her hand – it seemed bound to her side. 'Give me Your forgiveness,' she prayed. 'I cannot forgive him on my own.' As she took his hand, Corrie felt an amazing current passing from herself to him, and love filled her heart. 'So,' she concluded, 'I discovered that when God tells us to love our enemies, he gives, along with the command, the love itself.
Anon

COMMENT   From time to time we all do things which need forgiving. We must be prepared to say sorry and to ask forgiveness – when we know we have done wrong. And offer forgiveness to others, when they have hurt us.

SCRIPTURE READING   Matthew 18:21-22 (or *New World*, page 64)

PRAYER   Dear God,
I find it so hard to forgive those who are unkind to me,
or who blame me for things which are not my fault.
I go on bearing a grudge against them,
and even when they try to make it up
I feel bitter and hard.
I know this is wrong.
When Peter asked Jesus how many times
he ought to forgive someone who had wronged him,
Jesus said he must go on and on forgiving.
Jesus even prayed for forgiveness
for those who crucified him.
Please help me to be more like him
and be willing to forgive.
Amen.
Nancy Martin

HYMN   Make me a channel of your peace (HON/Source)

ALTERNATIVES

HYMN   It's me, it's me, it's me, O Lord (HON)

READING   See Additional readings, number 9 (page 122)

PRAYERS   See assembly A3 or E44

D34 Temptation

HYMN	Be still, and know that I am God (HON)
COMMENT	Let us think for a moment of the sea. Some of you might be imagining a clear, blue, peaceful sea, as we see it in the summer holiday brochures; some may be remembering winter storms shown on TV news, when coastal towns were battered and ships were in distress.
SCRIPTURE READING	Mark 4:35-41 (or *New World*, page 13)
COMMENT	The friends of Jesus were terrified of the stormy sea; they were tempted to doubt – they lacked faith.
READING	*Light shining out of darkness*

God moves in a mysterious way
his wonders to perform;
he plants his footsteps in the sea,
and rides upon the storm.

Deep in unfathomable mines
of never-failing skill
he treasures up his bright designs,
and works his sovereign will.

Ye fearful saints fresh courage take;
the clouds ye so much dread
are big with mercy, and shall break
in blessings on your head.

Judge not the Lord by feeble sense,
but trust him for his grace;
behind a frowning providence
he hides a smiling face.

His purposes will ripen fast
unfolding every hour;
the bud may have a bitter taste,
but sweet will be the flower.

Blind belief is sure to err,
and scan his work in train;
God is his own interpreter,
and he will make it plain.
William Cowper

PRAYER   Lord Jesus, I have watched the sea
when I have been to the coast on holiday.
Even in summer, the waves pound the beach
and hiss over the shingle as if they were living, angry things.

I have watched the sea on the television news in winter
when great breakers have pounded the promenades
and tossed cars about as if with a giant hand.

I'm always a bit afraid of the sea, Lord,
even in its summer moods.

Yet you could stand erect in a heaving boat
and command the tumbling waves to be still.
No wonder your disciples were amazed.
What courage you showed!

Please share that courage with me, Lord Jesus.
Great waves of temptation bear against the shores of my heart.
Help me to still the storm,
and bring me to the safe harbour of your peace.
Mary Drewery

HYMN   Peace, perfect peace (HON)

ALTERNATIVES

HYMN   Lord, for tomorrow (HON)

PRAYERS   O Lord God, grant us always,
whatever the world may say,
to be concerned about what you will say,
and to care only for your approval,
which will outweigh all words;
for Jesus Christ's sake.
Amen.
General Gordon

See also assembly A3 or C24

D35 God with us

HYMN   Immortal, invisible, God only wise (HON/Source)

COMMENT   It's easy to think of God as a fearful, faraway figure who is not very interested in us. Too distant and remote to be approached. This is what Jimmy Savile says about fearing God.

READING   God does not frighten me in the way that a horror film does. God, however, does fill me with complete respect. You see, I am in the business of kidding people in a very light-hearted way. I am rather like a magician who will, by sleight of hand, deceive you. Or I am like a clown, who by purposeful and very carefully thought-out blunderings makes you laugh. I am both the deceiver, in the best sense, I hope – and a blunderer with words. I think that I can turn most people on when I start with my light-hearted words and such-like. But I have to be very careful because if I ever slipped up and thought I could deceive God, then my whole world would be worth nothing. I have no need to be afraid of God; you have no need to be afraid of God. Neither of us need be afraid of anything. But God has my complete respect. You see, God is impossible to kid.

As a matter of fact, I actually enjoy God because I have come to terms with that fact – that God cannot be kidded.
Jimmy Savile

COMMENT   God can't be kidded – it means it's not a matter of fearing God but respecting him, for he is so close to us that he knows us inside out.

SCRIPTURE READING   Psalm 139:1-14 (or *Winding Quest*, page 402)

PRAYER   Christ be with me,
Christ within me,
Christ behind me,
Christ before me,
Christ beside me,
Christ to win me,
Christ to comfort and restore me,
Christ beneath me,
Christ above me,
Christ in quiet and
Christ in danger,
Christ in hearts of all that love me,
Christ in mouth of friend and stranger.
St Patrick

HYMN   Make me a channel of your peace (HON/Source)

ALTERNATIVES

HYMN   He's got the whole world in his hand (HON)

PRAYERS   See assembly A4 or A9 (alternative prayers)

WORLD RELIGIOUS THEMES

E36 Creation

HYMN   Morning has broken (HON)

COMMENT   'Like the first morning', the hymn said. Do we appreciate the beauty of the world God has created for us; that on the very first morning of the world's existence God started his work of creation?

READING 1   A little girl who lived in a remote part of the country was receiving her first introduction to the Bible from her elderly grandmother, and the old lady was reading the child the story of creation. After the story had been finished the little girl seemed lost in thought. 'Well, dear,' said the grandmother, 'what do you think of it?' 'Oh, I love it. It's so exciting,' exclaimed the youngster. 'You never know what God is going to do next!'
Anon

COMMENT   The little girl was quite right – you never know what God is going to do next. Each day his work of creation continues – with the birth of every new baby, the opening of each fragile flower, the invention of new computers and the discovery of medical techniques and cures. God's work of creation continues each day.

READING 2   In a little church in the far south of Ireland, every window but one is of stained glass, representing Christ and his saints. Through the one window which is plain glass may be seen a breathtaking view: a lake of deepest blue, studded with green islets and backed by range after range of purple hills. Under the window is the inscription: 'The heavens declare the glory of God, and the firmament showeth his handiwork.'
Robert Gibbings

COMMENT   Let us pause in silence to think of God's great power – that power which can create galaxies in outer space and tiny daisies in our fields.

PRAYER O God, we thank you for this earth, our home;
for the wide sky and the blessed sun,
for the salt sea and the running water,
for the everlasting hills and the never-resting winds,
for trees and the common grass underfoot.
We thank you for our senses
by which we hear the songs of birds,
and see the splendour of the summer fields,
and taste of the autumn fruits,
and rejoice in the feel of the snow,
and smell the breath of the spring.
Grant us a heart wide open to all this beauty
and save our souls from being so blind
that we pass unseeing when even the common thorn-bush
is aflame with your glory;
O God, our Creator,
who lives and reigns for ever and ever.
Amen.
Walter Rauschenbusch

HYMN Now thank we all our God (HON)

ALTERNATIVES

HYMNS All things bright and beautiful (HON/Source)
O Lord, my God (HON/Source)
All creatures of our God and King (HON)

READING See Additional readings, number 15 (page 124)

PRAYERS For eyes whereby I clearly see
the many lovely things there be;
for lungs to breathe the morning air,
for nose to smell its fragrance rare;
for tongue to taste the fruits that grow,
for birds that sing and flowers that blow;
for limbs to climb, and swing, and run,
for skin to feel the cheerful sun;
for sun and moon and stars in heaven,
whose gracious light is freely given;
the river where the green weed floats,
and where I sail my little boats;
the sea where I can bathe and play,
the sands where I can race all day;
the pigeons wheeling in the sun,
who fly more quickly than I run;
the winds that sing as they rush by,

the clouds that race across the sky;
the shelter of the shady woods,
where I may spend my lonely moods;
the gabled house that is my home,
the garden where I love to roam;
and bless my parents, every day,
though they be very far away;
take thou my thanks, O God above,
for all these tokens of thy love.
And when I am a man do thou
make me as grateful then as now.
Richard Molesworth Dennis
(a soldier poet who died in the First World War)

See also assembly G54

E37 Supreme Being

HYMN   Immortal, invisible, God only wise (HON/Source)

COMMENT   This hymn emphasises the infinite, awe-inspiring power and splendour of God; but this is the same God that Jesus called 'Abba', which we would translate as 'Daddy'.

SCRIPTURE READING   Luke 10:21-22 (or *New World*, page 98, 5 and 6)

COMMENT   One of Jesus' most important tasks was to make this God better known, respected and loved.

READING   I offer you
every flower that ever grew,
every bird that ever flew,
every wind that ever blew.
Good God!

Every thunder rolling,
every church bell tolling,
every leaf and sod.
We praise you!

I offer you
every wave that ever moved,
every heart that ever loved,
you, your Father's Well-Beloved.
Dear Lord.

Every river dashing,
every lightning flashing,
like an angel's sword.
We bless you!

I offer you
every cloud that ever swept
o'er the skies, and broke and wept
in rain, and with the flowerets slept.
My King!

Each communicant praying,
every angel staying,
before your throne to sing.
We adore you!

I offer you
every flake of virgin snow,
every spring of earth below,
every human joy and woe.
My love!

O Lord! And all your glorious
self o'er death victorious,
throned in heaven above.
We glorify you!
Ancient Irish prayer

PRAYER   Supreme Lord and Father,
we praise you for your creation,
we adore you as your creatures,
we bless you for all the good you shower on us,
we glorify you for the death and resurrection of your Son,
we love and thank you for your constant care of us.
All this we express through Christ your Son.
Amen.

HYMN   O Lord, my God (HON / Source)

ALTERNATIVES

HYMNS   All creatures of our God and King (HON)
Now thank we all our God (HON)

PRAYERS   See assembly E36 (either prayer)

E38 Worship

HYMN   All people that on earth do dwell (HON/Source)

COMMENT   This assembly has as its theme 'worship', the very thing that we try to do each time we gather here for prayers. The hymn we have just sung says, 'his praise forth tell', which means 'let's give a lot of praise and thanks to God'. And that is what worship is.

READING 1   It is a law of man's nature, written into his very essence, and just as much a part of him as the desire to build houses and cultivate the land and marry and have children and read books and sing songs, that he should want to stand together with other people in order to acknowledge their common dependence on God, their Father and Creator.
Thomas Merton

READING 2   God is the supreme artist. He loves to have things beautiful. Look at the sunset and flowers and the snow-capped mountains and the stars. They are beautiful because they come from God. God loves to have things beautiful in church, too. And the same goes for church courtesies. To show our reverence for the cross on which he died for us, and for the Sacrament in which he comes to our hearts, is just to be polite to God. This is not required, but it is the part of Christian good breeding. It has the importance that courtesy has the world over.
John S. Baldwin

COMMENT   Saying 'thank you' to God is one way of praising and worshipping him, for by our gratitude for what he has done for us we are showing how much we depend on him and love him.

PRAYER   O God, thank you for making me as I am.
Thank you for health and strength,
for eyes to see;
for ears to hear;
for hands to work;
for feet to walk and run.
For a mind to think;
for a memory to remember;
for a heart to love.
Thank you for
parents who are kind to me;
friends who are true to me;

teachers who are patient with me.
Thank you for this wonderful life.
Help me to try to deserve all your gifts a little more.
This I ask for Jesus' sake.
Amen.
William Barclay

HYMN   Majesty, worship his majesty (HON)

ALTERNATIVES

HYMNS   Praise to the Lord, the Almighty (HON)
Praise, my soul, the King of heaven (HON/Source)
Give me joy in my heart (HON)

PRAYERS   O God, who has made this great world,
the sun and the moon and the stars;
we thank you for this wonderful earth,
filled with all that we need for life.
Teach us how to discover
what is good and useful for everyone.
Bless what people have invented and use
so that there is enough for everyone's need.
Amen.
R. S. Macnicol

See also assembly E36

E39 Prayer

HYMN O the love of my Lord (HON)

COMMENT There is a story of a priest (minister) who asked a little boy if he said his prayers each night. The boy said, 'Yes.' 'Do you say them in the morning?' the priest (minister) asked. 'No,' said the lad, 'I ain't scared in the daytime!'

Do we say prayers just because it's a habit or we're afraid not to – just in case something should happen to us if we don't? Prayer should be like talking to our friends. But it's not easy to do that.

READING 1 While journeying on horseback one day, St Benedict met a peasant walking along the road. 'You've got an easy job,' said the peasant. 'Why don't I become a man of prayer? Then I too would be travelling on horseback.' 'You think praying is easy,' replied the Saint. 'If you can say the Lord's Prayer once without any distraction you can have this horse. 'It's a bargain,' said the surprised peasant.

Closing his eyes and folding his hands he began to say the Lord's Prayer aloud: 'Our Father, who art in heaven, hallowed be thy name, thy kingdom come . . .' Suddenly he stopped and looked up. 'Will I get the saddle and bridle too?'
Anon

COMMENT It's easy to be distracted while praying – prayer needs not only effort, to keep trying, but also love. We need to make a loving effort.

READING 2 One day a mother noticed that her little girl was in her room a long time and she had said she was going to pray to Jesus. Finally when the little girl came out her mother asked her what she was doing in her room for such a long time when she had just gone in to pray. 'I was just telling Jesus that I love him and he was telling me that he loves me. And we were just loving each other.'
Anon

PRAYER Dear Lord Jesus, teach us to be generous,
to serve you as you deserve,
to give and not to count the cost,
to fight and not to heed the wounds,
to toil and not to seek for rest,
to labour and ask for no reward
save that of knowing that we do your will.
Amen.
St Ignatius Loyola

Hymn   O Lord, all the world belongs to you (HON)

ALTERNATIVES

Hymns   Rejoice in the Lord always (HON)
Be still and know that I am God (HON/Source)

Prayer   See assembly E18

E40 Fasting

HYMN It's me, O Lord (HON)

COMMENT For the Christian, suggestions of fasting turn our thoughts to the season of Lent – although fasting is not limited to a season.

READING The Saxons called March 'lencten monath' because in this month the days noticeably lengthen. As the chief part of the great fast, from Ash Wednesday to Easter, falls in March, it received the name Lencten-Faesren or Lent. The fast of 36 days was introduced in the fourth century, but it did not become fixed at 40 days until the early seventh century, thus corresponding with Our Lord's fast in the wilderness.
Anon

COMMENT Our example and inspiration for the self-discipline of fasting comes from Jesus himself.

SCRIPTURE READING Luke 4:1-13

PRAYER Lord Jesus, we are thinking of you in the desert.
We remember that for forty days and forty nights
you were tempted there to disobey God's will.
You know how often we are tempted to do wrong.
Please show us how to overcome our temptations
as you overcame your own.
Help us to be strong-minded
and teach us to banish wrong thoughts when they come.
Make us true and brave and more like you every day.
Amen.
Brenda Holloway

HYMN God forgave my sin (HON/Source)

ALTERNATIVES

HYMNS The Lord's my shepherd (HON/Source)
Forty days and forty nights (HON)

PRAYERS   Forgive me
when I ask you for too much –
when I forget to thank you for what I already have.
Forgive me, too, when I am selfish and demanding –
When I want to *get* more than I want to *give*.
Amen.
Brother Kenneth and Sister Geraldine

See also assembly E18

E41 Care for others

HYMN   I, the Lord of sea and sky (HON/Source)

COMMENT   There is a beautiful English proverb that says, 'He who plants trees loves others more than himself.'

READING 1   Over 10,000 people in Provence, France, owe their homes and environment to a little-known peasant shepherd. Elezard Bouffier lived alone in 1910 in a barren region where there were very few trees. While tending his flocks in the autumn, the shepherd would pick up each acorn that he saw. In the early spring, while watching the sheep, he would prod the earth with his staff and drop in a nut. He did this each year between 1910 and 1947. At his death, the barren countryside was covered by trees and teeming with wildlife. It is now the pleasant site of a new housing development.
Anon

COMMENT   It is so often the little things in life that count. Most of us hardly notice trees at all – but they can inspire poetry and thoughts of God.

READING 2   I think that I shall never see
a poem lovely as a tree.

A tree whose hungry mouth is prest
against the earth's sweet flowing breast;

a tree that looks at God all day,
and lifts her leafy arms to pray;

a tree that may in summer wear
a nest of robins in her hair;

upon whose bosom snow has lain;
who intimately lives with rain.

Poems are made by fools like me,
but only God can make a tree.
Joyce Kilmer

PRAYER   To pull up or destroy a tree, Lord,
is to destroy something that you have created.
It is to rob birds of a home,
to take away shade,
to make the landscape barren.
To plant a tree, or respect its growth,

is to work with God the creator,
to provide homes and shelter for birds,
to share with generations not yet born
a thing of beauty.
Lord, help us always to respect what you have made
and work with you in the masterpiece of your Creation.
Amen.

HYMN   Let there be love shared among us (HON/Source)

ALTERNATIVES

HYMNS   Praise him (HON)
All the nations of the earth (HON)

PRAYERS   See assembly E36 (either prayer)

E42 Inner light

HYMN	The Spirit lives to set us free (HON)
COMMENT	Have you ever been to a cathedral and admired the stained-glass windows? Chartres Cathedral in France has 175 magnificent windows. They were the first high-quality windows ever to be made and are still considered to be the best in the world. Their beauty and artistry can be appreciated only if you are inside when the sun pours through them, or outside when bright lights shine out from within the cathedral.
READING	People are like stained glass; they sparkle and shine when the sun is out, but when the darkness sets in, their true beauty is revealed only if there is light from within. *Elisabeth Kubler-Ross*
SCRIPTURE READINGS (2 READERS)	**A** Matthew 6:22-23 **B** Matthew 5:14-16
COMMENT	After hearing the words about the light within us, let us hear our first reading again, and think more deeply about its meaning.
READING	Repeat first reading
PRAYER	Come, Holy Spirit, light up our minds with your fire; destroy the darkness of selfishness that lurks within us. May we be so aglow with your love that people may see the good we do and give glory to the Father. We ask this through Christ, the Light of the World. Amen.
HYMN	Lord, the light of your love (HON)

ALTERNATIVES

HYMNS	Make me a channel of your peace (HON/Source) I watch the sunrise (HON)
READINGS	See Additional readings, number 6 (page 120)
PRAYER	See assembly D27

E43 Judgement

HYMN   Lord, for tomorrow (HON)

READING   The Irish have a story of an Irishman who appeared before St Peter expecting admission, and when his ledger showed pages and pages of heavy debit entries, said that the books had been badly kept, for he knew he had once given twopence to a beggar. St Peter, after much flipping over of pages, found it so indeed; but was twopence sufficient to outweigh all else? Then the Irishman said he had a friend called Patrick. If they would have the common politeness to call him he would make it all right. St Patrick was summoned, looked at the ledger, and he and St Peter exchanged doubtful glances. 'What are we to do with this countryman of yours?' asked St Peter. 'You see how it is.' 'Yes,' said St Patrick, 'I see how it is. Give him back his twopence!'
Anon

COMMENT   The hymn we sang reminded us that it's what we do today that matters; it is no good promising about tomorrow if we make no effort today. The reading, in a humorous way, draws our attention to the fact that we will be judged on what we have done.

SCRIPTURE READING   Matthew 25:31-46 (or *New World*, page 100)

PRAYER   Lift up our hearts, O Christ,
above the false show of things,
above laziness and fear,
above selfishness and covetousness,
above custom and fashion,
up to the everlasting Truth that you are;
so that we may live joyfully and freely,
in the faith that you are our King and our Saviour,
our Example and our Judge,
and that, as long as we are loyal to you
all will be well with us in this world
and in all worlds to come.
Amen.

HYMN   Do not be afraid (HON)

ALTERNATIVES

PRAYERS   See assembly A4 or E44

E44 Everlasting life

HYMN	Crown him with many crowns (HON/Source)
COMMENT	'Thy praise shall never, never fail throughout eternity.' Have you noticed how many prayers and hymns end with words like 'for ever and ever, Amen' and similar references to life after death, eternity, or everlasting life? This is sometimes called 'heaven'. Listen to what some famous people have said about heaven.
READINGS (4 READERS)	**A** *Confucius* said, 'Heaven means to be one with God.' **B** *Thomas Hardy* said, 'The main object of religion is not to get a person into heaven, but to get heaven into him.' **C** *Joseph Addison* said, 'Heaven is not to be looked upon only as a reward, but as the natural effect of a good life.' **D** *Dante* said, 'If you insist on having your own way, you will get it. Hell is the enjoyment of your own way for ever. If you really want God's way with you, you will get it in heaven.'
SCRIPTURE READING	John 14:14
PRAYER	All that we ought to have thought and have not thought, all that we ought to have said and have not said, all that we ought to have done and have not done, all that we ought not to have thought and yet have thought, all that we ought not to have spoken and yet have spoken, all that we ought not to have done and yet have done, for these words and works pray we, O God, for forgiveness, and repent with penance. Amen. *The Zendavesta, ascribed to Zoroaster, about 700 BC*
HYMN	Morning has broken (HON)

ALTERNATIVES

HYMNS	For all the saints (HON) The King of love my shepherd is (HON)
PRAYERS	See assembly D27 or E43

E45 Happiness

HYMN   Give me joy in my heart (HON)

COMMENT   Happiness is what you and I and every human person seeks and longs for.

READING   There was a medieval king who regularly used the advice of a wise man. This old man was summoned to the king's presence. The monarch asked him how to get rid of his anxiety and depression, how he might be really happy, for he was sick in body and mind. The wise man replied, 'There is but one cure for the king. Your Majesty must sleep one night in the shirt of a happy man.'

Messengers were despatched throughout the realm to search for a man who was truly happy. But everyone who was approached had some cause for misery, something that robbed them of true and complete happiness. At last they found a man – a poor beggar – who sat smiling by the roadside and, when they asked him if he was really happy and had no sorrows, he confessed that he was a truly happy man. Then they told him what they wanted. The king must sleep one night in the shirt of a happy man, and had given them a large sum of money to procure such a shirt. Would he sell them his shirt that the king might wear it? The beggar burst into uncontrollable laughter and replied, 'I am sorry I cannot oblige the king. I haven't a shirt on my back.'
Anon

COMMENT   Often people are unhappy because they want to be what they are not; they haven't learnt to accept themselves as they are – they want to live in an unreal world, a dream world, a world of their fantasies.

SCRIPTURE READING   Matthew 5:1-10 (or *New World*, page 102)

PRAYER   Father Almighty,
you made us to be happy,
to be one with you;
but when sin entered the world
that happiness was frustrated.
We all long to be happy,
but it is all too easy to look for happiness in the wrong places.
Please help each of us to seek happiness
through kindness and service to others.
We ask this through Christ your Son.
Amen.

HYMN Be still and know that I am God (HON/Source)

ALTERNATIVES

HYMNS Let there be love shared among us (HON/Source)
Love divine, all loves excelling (HON/Source)

PRAYERS See assembly D35 or G54

FAMILY AND PEOPLE GROUPS

F46 Family

HYMN Bind us together, Lord (HON/Source)

COMMENT The opening song reminds us that we are bound together in love to our family and friends. It's usually little things that bind us together in a family – the familiar ordinary things.

READING 1 A glimpse of a pram through the window,
a whistle from Auntie Bee;
a rat-rat at the letter box,
and the cousins are here for tea.
Marion is bald, as babies are,
Peter has short red hair;
Mother takes charge of Marion,
but Peter falls to my share.
Now the bricks go back to the cupboard,
and we settle down to our teas,
And I'll tell you something peculiar:
Peter likes jam with his cheese.
J. Walsh

COMMENT We don't just belong to a family; we have duties and responsibilities in our family life. We are each in one another's care.

READING 2 A well-timed bite by a four-year-old girl, with a good sense of smell, saved her family from gas poisoning. A peculiar odour awakened the child at 3 o'clock one morning and she hurried to her father's room to tell him. When a vigorous shake failed to disturb his peaceful slumber, she bit him on the arm. That did the trick. The police discovered that the strange smell was caused by monoxide fumes from the family car which had been left running in the adjoining garage. The parents and all three children were in good condition after being administered a dose of oxygen.
Anon

PRAYER   Let us give thanks to God
for our homes and families.
May we grow in appreciation
of all that we have been given
in love and material blessings
over the years.
May we be kept from treating our homes
as lodging houses
and from showing insufficient concern for our parents.
As we thank God for our homes
we pray for all the homeless throughout the world.
We think of all the refugees
– keep their distress in our minds –
it is so easy for 'refugee' to become just a word to us.
We make this prayer in the name of Jesus
who lived in a family in Nazareth.
Amen.
K. A. Clegg

HYMN   Father, I place into your hands (HON/Source)

ALTERNATIVES

HYMNS   Love is his word (HON)
Now thank we all our God (HON)

PRAYERS   See assembly D31

F47 God has no favourites

HYMN   O Lord, all the world belongs to you (verses 1 to 3) (HON)

COMMENT   'We are one body in this one Lord.' We are God's people, members of his family, and therefore brothers and sisters. In his family God has no favourites – he doesn't prefer people of one colour to people of another, and he's not interested in which country we live in, or whether we are male or female, rich or poor.

SCRIPTURE READING   Romans 2:6-11 (or *New World*, page 297)

COMMENT   God does not see the colour of our skin, or whether we are popular with others or not. God has no enemies and no favourites.

READING   (This reading is taken from Ernest Gordon's account of life in a Japanese prison camp during the Second World War. What you are about to hear takes place towards the end of the prisoners' captivity, after they have been released from being very brutally treated by their Japanese captors.)

Farther on, we were shunted on to a siding for a lengthy stay. We found ourselves on the same track with several carloads of Japanese wounded. They were on their own and without medical care. No longer fit for action, they had been packed into railway trucks which were being returned to Bangkok. Whenever one of them died en route, he was thrown off into the jungle. The ones who survived to reach Bangkok would presumably receive some form of medical treatment there. But they were given none on the way. They were in a shocking state; I have never seen men filthier. Their uniforms were encrusted with mud, blood and excrement. Their wounds, sorely inflamed and full of pus, crawled with maggots. . . . Without a word most of the officers in my section unbuckled their packs, took out part of their ration and a rag or two, and with water canteens in their hands went over to the Japanese train to help them. Our guards tried to prevent us, bawling, 'No goodka! No goodka!' But we ignored them and knelt by the side of the enemy to give them food and water, to clean and bind their wounds, to smile and say a kind word. Grateful cries of 'Aragatto' (thank you) followed us when we left. An allied officer from another section of the train had been taking it all in. 'What bloody fools you all are!' he said to me. 'Don't you realise that those are the enemy?'
Ernest Gordon

PRAYER Almighty God,
we know that you love everyone
and have no favourites.
Help us to be like you,
to treat everyone with care and kindness,
especially those we find it difficult to get on with.
We ask you this through your Son, Jesus,
who died for everyone
regardless of their colour or creed.
Amen.

HYMN From heaven you came (The Servant King) (HON/Source)

ALTERNATIVES

HYMN A new commandment (HON/Source)

READING See Additional readings, number 20 (page 126)

PRAYERS See assembly A6 or A3

F48 Refugees

HYMN When I needed a neighbour (HON)

COMMENT Whenever there's a war, there are people fleeing from the fighting area – refugees. When people are deprived of their freedom, they try to escape to where they can be free.

READING
(2 READERS)

Simon My name is Simon and I came to the camp in 1989 when it first opened . . . two of my children were born here and know nothing else. Now we are being told we can go back to our homes and I have great hopes that we will be able to return, but I don't think it's safe yet. The roads are still mined.

Zacaria (Simon's wife) *(interrupts)* How can we walk down roads which are mined? How can we drive in a lorry when it might be blown up at any time? Many people in Mozambique have only one leg because they trod on an anti-personnel mine.

Simon *(continues)* I want to start my life again. I need money, I need food for the journey, but most of all we need peace.

Zacaria Then we could go home safely and start our lives again.

COMMENT For many years the Jewish people, God's chosen people, lived as exiles, or refugees, in a foreign land. They thanked God for his goodness, but longed to return home.

PRAYER Teach us, O Lord,
to hope in your Name,
which is the source and fount of all creation.
Open the eyes of our hearts to know you,
who alone are Highest amid the highest,
and ever abide Holy amidst the holy.
Deliver the afflicted, pity the lowly,
raise the fallen, reveal yourself to the needy,
heal the sick, and bring home your wandering people.
Feed the hungry, ransom the captive,
support the weak, comfort the faint-hearted.
Let all the nations of the earth
know that you are God alone,
that Jesus Christ is your child,
and that we are your people

and the sheep of your pasture.
To you, who alone can grant to us
these and other yet more excellent benefits,
we offer our praises through Jesus Christ,
the High Priest and Guardian of our souls;
through whom be glory and majesty to you
now and for all generations and unto ages of ages.
Amen.
Clement of Rome

HYMN   God's Spirit is in my heart (HON)

ALTERNATIVES

HYMN   From heaven you came (The Servant King) (HON/Source)

PRAYER   Lord Jesus,
we remember how, when you were born,
there was no place in all the town of Bethlehem
to lay a baby down.
Take now into your loving care
all homeless children everywhere.
And we remember how, at Galilee,
the waiting crowd by a miracle was fed,
on two small fishes and five leaves of bread.
Lord Jesus, listen to our prayer,
feed hungry children everywhere.
Amen.
Sally Cawley

F49 Travelling people – Gypsies

HYMN   All people that on earth do dwell (HON/Source)

COMMENT   The hymn we have just sung opens with the words, 'All people', and that would include one of the most disrespected groups in the country – the travelling people, in the past called gypsies. They often suffer from prejudice and discrimination.

READING 1   The village folk of Stephen's Green, Kent, are up in arms again over gypsies. Six of the estimated 7,000 travelling families in the country camped last Friday on the wide grass verge alongside the A25, on the west side of the station. The parish council summoned an emergency meeting last night to seek ways of moving the gypsies on and stopping their return. Councillor Carter's boldly proposed idea of seeking land for a permanent site for them was rejected out of hand. Mr Carter had tried to point out that the Caravan Site Act of Parliament encouraged the setting up of sites for the travelling families. Councillor Carter accused the parish council of acting in a very un-Christian fashion, as they sought ways to hound the gypsies from the area.
Anon

COMMENT   The United Nations Charter of Human Rights declares, 'All human beings are born free and equal in dignity and rights.' A Christian would put it this way:

READING 2   We are no longer outsiders and foreigners in God's world; we are fellow-citizens with all the friends of Jesus everywhere and members of God's family.
Alan Dale

PRAYER   We pray for those who feel isolated and neglected.
ALL   We are members of God's family
and pray for them.

We pray for the persecuted, the unwanted, the refugees.
ALL   We are members of God's family
and pray for them.

We pray for the minority groups throughout the world
and especially for gypsies in this country.
ALL   We are members of God's family
and pray for them.

HYMN   Bind us together, Lord (HON/Source)

ALTERNATIVES

HYMNS   A new commandment (HON/Source)
Love is his word (HON)

PRAYER   See assembly A8

F50 The hungry

HYMN	God's Spirit is in my heart (HON)

SCRIPTURE READING   Mark 6:35-44 (or *New World*, page 25)

COMMENT   In that reading we heard how concerned Jesus was for those who were hungry. Many agencies and individuals today work to relieve the undernourished.

READING 1   Many years ago, during the Second World War, a group of people in Oxford got together to send aid to children starving in Greece. They called themselves the Oxford Committee for Famine Relief and before long they were known as Oxfam. Their work spread: from Oxford to many other towns and cities; from helping Greek children to any group in need. Thousands of volunteers collected money through fundraising events, shops were opened to sell second-hand clothes, and every possible method of raising money was used. Oxfam became world-famous for its relief work.

READING 2   Mother Teresa of Calcutta died only a few days after the tragic death of Diana, Princess of Wales. They were different in so many ways, but united in their deep desire to help the poor and the hungry. They met several times and there are many photographs of them hand in hand together. Mother Teresa's last public appearance and statement, just before her own death, was made to acknowledge publicly Princess Diana's love for the poor.
Anon

READER 3   Mother Teresa had once advised Princess Diana that when she was suffering or in distress, she should reach out to others who were suffering, and she would find that they in turn reached out to her. The immense outpouring of affection that marked the funeral of Diana was to provide tangible evidence of the truth of those words.
Kathryn Spink, biography of Mother Teresa

PRAYER   Lord Jesus,
we remember how you were concerned for and fed
a waiting crowd of people in Galilee.
Bless and help all those agencies and individuals
who show your concern for the hungry of our world.
Help us, too, to do all we can to share your concern.
Amen.

HYMN   When I needed a neighbour (HON)

ALTERNATIVES

HYMNS   For the healing of the nations (HON)
              O Lord, all the world belongs to you (HON)

PRAYER   See assembly E38 (alternative prayer)

F51 Elderly people

HYMN	Lord, for tomorrow (HON)

SCRIPTURE READINGS
(4 READERS)

A Even to your old age and grey hairs I am he, I am he who will sustain you. I have made you and I will carry you; I will sustain you and I will rescue you. *Isaiah 46:4*

B They will still bear fruit in old age, they will stay fresh and green ... *Psalm 92:14*

C Teach us to number our days aright, that we may gain a heart of wisdom. *Psalm 90:12*

D He seldom reflects on the days of his life, because God keeps him occupied with gladness of heart. *Ecclesiastes 5:20*

COMMENT Old age is a time for wisdom, for maturity – an opportunity to rest from the hard work of a lifetime and grow closer to God.

SCRIPTURE READING John 2:10

PRAYER
Dear Father,
we pray for all old people.
Help us to respect them
as people who have lived through childhood and youth.
Most of them have had families
and are now grandparents or great-grandparents.
Help us to respect them as mature adults
who have grown in wisdom with the passing of the years.
Comfort those who are sick, tired or lonely.
Help us always to be thoughtful and considerate
when we meet them,
for they are special in your eyes.
We ask you this through Jesus your Son.
Amen.

HYMN The Lord's my shepherd (HON/Source)

ALTERNATIVES

HYMNS Lord of all hopefulness (HON)
God is love (HON)

PRAYERS See assembly A9 (alternative prayer)

F52 Street children

HYMN   Do not be afraid (HON)

READER   Read the last three verses of the hymn.

COMMENT   To a child living on the streets of a Third World city those words would mean a great deal. God is on their side; each street child is precious in God's eyes.

SCRIPTURE READING   **A** Mark 9:36-37
(2 READERS)   **B** Mark 10:13-16

READING   There are about 11,000 children between the ages of 5 and 17 living, working and sleeping on the streets of Accra, the capital of Ghana. This is a true story about one of them.

Kwame is a 14-year-old shoe-shine boy. He sleeps each night at the lorry park of Accra, under one of the lorries for shelter. He wakes as soon as it gets light and buys some water from the local water lorry to wash with. By 6.30 am Kwame will be looking for the women who sell food on the streets. If he has kept enough money from the day before he will buy some rice water or porridge, and a piece of bread. Then he will join the crowds heading for the city centre with his precious box of shoe-shining materials under his arm. He has his own patch of pavement but may have to fight another boy to drive him off, to protect his area.

Kwame will be there all day, through the terrible humid heat of the day. If he has a good day he may earn the equivalent of £1; if he has a bad day he will be hungry. Like most poor people, Kwame spends 70 per cent of what he earns on food and water. He finishes as it gets dark and heads back to the lorry park. Chances are that he will be fast asleep by 10 o'clock, having first paid for water to wash and to use a toilet. He will also pay a watchman to guard his shoe-shine box while he is asleep under a lorry. (Some street boys earn money by staying awake all night guarding the shoe-shine boys' boxes.)

PRAYER   Heavenly Father,
who loves all children and young people,
it is hard to take in and realise
that people like us live all their lives –

every minute of every day and night –
on the pavements and alleyways of towns and cities,
with nowhere to eat, sleep, watch TV,
or do any of the things that we do every day.
We pray that more and more people
will realise how terrible this is
and work to end such misery and injustice.
Amen.

HYMN   When I needed a neighbour (HON)

ALTERNATIVES

HYMNS   A new commandment (HON/Source)

READING   See Additional readings, number 24 (page 127)

PRAYER   O Divine Master, grant that I may seek not so much
to be consoled, as to console,
to be understood, as to understand,
to be loved, as to love;
for it is in giving that we receive,
it is in pardoning that we are pardoned,
and it is in dying that we are born to
eternal life.
Amen.
St Francis of Assisi

F53 Option for the poor

HYMN   I, the Lord of sea and sky (HON/Source)

COMMENT   Let us take a closer look at the words we have just sung.

READER A   I, the Lord of sea and sky,
I have heard my people cry.
All who dwell in dark and sin
my hand will save.

COMMENT   Who are those who live in the dark? The Creator says, 'I have heard their cry.'

READER B   To live in the dark is to live without hope.
To live in the dark is to be without what is basic to life.
To live in the dark is to be so poor that you have –
insufficient food;
insufficient housing;
insufficient health care;
insufficient education.
To live in the dark is to live without hope.
Anon

READER A   I, the Lord of snow and rain,
I have borne my people's pain.
I have wept for love of them.

COMMENT   When God himself became one of us, a human person, he came as a poor man, who lived his whole life among the poor. God experienced poverty and the arrogance of the rich.

READER B   Luke 20:45-21:4

READER A   I, the Lord of wind and flame,
I will tend the poor and lame.
I will set a feast for them.
My hand will save.

COMMENT   No one hearing these words or knowing the words of God in the Bible can doubt that God has a special love and concern for the poor. The Church has asked us to show the same special love – an option for the poor.

PRAYER   Lord, if I forget the poor
           because I am busy running around,
           if I close my eyes to their plight
           because I am anxious about my own life,
           forgive me,
           and help me to be more mindful in the future.

           Instil in me a deeper sense of your justice,
           so that I will never turn my back
           on your little ones,
           your hungry ones,
           your suffering ones.

           May I pay back your love to me
           with love to them.
           Amen.
           Patrick Sayles

HYMN   Sing the opening hymn again

           ALTERNATIVES

HYMNS   A new commandment (HON/Source)
           Let there be love shared among us (HON/Source)

READING   See Additional readings, numbers 10 (page 122), 12 (page 123) and
           14 (page 124)

PRAYER   You are Lord of the poor,
           Lord of the afflicted,
           Lord of the needy.
           May we praise you
           by sharing with the poor,
           by making them special in our lives,
           so that our time on earth be blessed,
           until it is finally fulfilled in your eternity.
           Amen.
           Patrick Sayles

GENERAL THEMES

G54 Thanksgiving

HYMN   Father, we adore you (HON)

SCRIPTURE READING   Luke 17:11-19 (or *New World*, page 145)

COMMENT   Of the ten healed only one returned to say, 'Thank you'. Jesus told us that we have much to learn from the simplicity of little children. Here are two stories from which we might learn.

READING 1   Little Karen was being taught that the proper thing to do was to write a 'thank you' letter to family and friends who had given her Christmas presents. She seemed to do pretty well until it came to Auntie Jane's gift. Finally she finished her note which read: 'Thank you for your Christmas present. I always wanted a toilet bag, although not very much.'
Anon

READING 2   A little girl was going to a party and her mother told her to be a good girl and remember to say 'thank you' to her hostess when leaving. When she got home her mother asked her if she had thanked the lady for the party. The little girl replied, 'Well, no. The girl in front of me did and the lady said, "Don't mention it" – so I didn't!'
Anon

COMMENT   Christians should have a 'thank you' attitude to life; always ready to thank God, because to say 'Thank you' is another way of saying 'We love you'.

PRAYER   For friends, who are always there,
Father, we thank you.
For the health that we all share,
Father, we thank you.

For CDs, sport and laughter,
Father, we thank you.
For McDonald's and burgers,
Father, we thank you.

For fashion, Nike and Reebok,
Father, we thank you.
For TV and *Star Trek*'s Spock,
Father, we thank you.

HYMN   Now thank we all our God (HON)

ALTERNATIVES

HYMNS   Praise, my soul, the King of heaven (HON/Source)
If I were a butterfly (HON)

PRAYERS   See assembly E36 (either prayer)

G55 Freedom

HYMN   Be still and know that I am God (HON/Source)

READING   Mother Teresa refused an offer of money from a rich Hindu gentle-
man to build a home for the dying. Why? Because he stipulated
that it must be a vegetarian house. Mother Teresa used to try to give
every dying person their last wish. Generally it is something like
water from the Ganges (for a Hindu); sometimes a cigarette or a
toffee apple; occasionally a chicken leg or wing. In a vegetarian
home she would not be able to give anyone chicken.
Anon

PRAYER   O God, within whose sight
all men have equal rights
to worship thee,
break every bar that holds
thy flock in diverse folds;
thy will from none withholds
full liberty.

Lord, set thy churches free
from foolish rivalry;
Lord, set us free!
Let all past bitterness
now and for ever cease,
and all our souls possess
thy charity!

Lord, set the people free!
Let all men draw to thee
in unity!
Thy temple courts are wide,
therein, let all abide
in peace, and side by side
serve only thee!

God, grant us now thy peace!
Bid all dissensions cease!
God, send us peace!
Peace in true liberty,
peace and fraternity,
God, send us peace!
John Oxenham

Hymn Bind us together, Lord (HON)

ALTERNATIVES

Hymns Peace, perfect peace (HON/Source)
Peace is flowing like a river (HON)

Prayer See assembly C24

G56 Hope

HYMN   Lord of all hopefulness (HON)

COMMENT   There is an old proverb that says, 'While there's life there's hope'. Too often people get discouraged when things get difficult, and just give up.

READING 1   Five times the athlete Diane Modahl was the British 800-metre champion runner. In 1994 she was sent home from the Commonwealth Games, held in Canada, in disgrace. Tests appeared to show that she had been taking performance-enhancing drugs and the Games officials banned her. Diane denied the charge and fought hard to clear her name and restore her reputation. It was over a year later that independent scientists proved that the Games officials, with their scientific tests, were wrong. Four years after her ordeal Diane spoke on TV and told how at her worst time, struggling with despair, she had put all her trust in God. She also told how she, and her Norwegian husband, named the baby girl that she had had at that time, *Imani*, which is the Norwegian for *Hope*.
Anon

READING 2   Do you know the story of the two frogs that fell into a bucket of cream? They tried hard to get out by climbing up the side of the bucket. But each time they slipped back again. Finally one frog said, 'We'll never get out of here. I give up.' So down he went and drowned. The other frog decided to keep trying. So again and again he tried to climb with his front legs and he kicked with his back legs. Suddenly he hit something hard. He turned to see what it was and discovered that all his kicking had churned up a lump of butter! He hopped on top of it and leaped out to safety.
Anon

COMMENT   Trying to overcome discouragement is hope in action; we must always be confident of God's caring love; there is a glorious future – just around the corner.

SCRIPTURE READING   Romans 8:18-25 (or *New World*, page 306)

PRAYER   Lord,
when things don't seem to be going very well,
and we are discouraged and fed up,
help us to place all our confidence in you.
Give us the patience we need

to trust in your loving care,
and please give us the gift of hope.
This we ask through Christ your Son.
Amen.

COMMENT   Although things went very badly for Jesus on the last day of his life, he never lost hope.

HYMN   I watch the sunrise (HON)

ALTERNATIVES

HYMN   God is love (HON)

G57 Stewardship of our planet

HYMN Morning has broken (HON)

COMMENT The opening words of our hymn remind us of the first morning of creation.

READING Genesis 1:1-5

COMMENT The light spoken of in our hymn and in the reading from Genesis is not as clear as it once was. Photographs taken of our planet, from space, show how the great forest fires in South America and other places are destroying the quality of the air.

READING Sweet the rain's new fall,
sunlit from heaven,
like the first dew-fall
on the first grass.

COMMENT Acid rain nowadays falls on the forests of Canada and Scandinavia destroying the woodlands and the animal and bird life of the forests.

READING Genesis 1:26-31

COMMENT God, the Creator, places all his creation into the hands of humans; not to kill, destroy and pollute, but to care for and be responsible for.

READING In the past fifty years, the earth has been destroyed and devastated more than in all the millions of years behind us. . . . If we want to live we have to do something immediately. . . . Let us always have the eyes of St Francis to see God in everything. And the heart St Francis had, to call all that is alive, all that can be developed or restored, our sisters and brothers.
Cardinal Arns of Brazil

PRAYER Father Creator,
we are so caught up in our own little lives and interests –
the here and the now –
that we take our planet-home for granted.
We too easily forget that you have entrusted us
with the care of your creation;
with the quality of the air,
the purity of the waters
and fertility of the soil.
May we become more conscious of our stewardship

and responsibility to care for our planet.
Help us to be faithful in small ways
and help others to come to an appreciation
of the danger our planet is in.
Amen.

HYMN   All the nations of the earth (HON)

ALTERNATIVES

HYMN   All things bright and beautiful (HON/Source)

READING   See Additional readings, numbers 13 (page 123) and 23 (page 127)

G58 Peace

HYMN Peace, perfect peace (HON/Source)

READING *Pax*

All that matters is to be one with the living God,
to be a creature
in the house of God of life.

Like a cat asleep on a chair
at peace, in peace
and at one with the master of the house,
with the mistress,
at home, at home in the house of the living,
sleeping on the hearth, and yawning before the fire.

Sleeping on the hearth of the living world,
yawning at home before the fire of life,
feeling the presence of the living God
like a great reassurance,
a deep calm in the heart,
a presence,
as of a master sitting at the board
in his own and greater being
in the house of life.
D. H. Lawrence

COMMENT True peace is a gift from God.

**SCRIPTURE READINGS
WITH PRAYER**
READER A 'Behold I stand at the door and knock. If anyone hears my voice and opens the door, I will come in to him and eat with him and he with me.'
Revelation 3:20

(short pause after each reading)

ALL Come, Lord, fill us with your peace.

READER B 'If a man loves me, he will keep my word, and my Father will love him, and we will come to him and make our home with him!'
John 14:23

ALL Come, Lord, fill us with your peace.

READER C   'Remain in me, and I in you. As the branch cannot bear fruit by itself, unless it is in the vine, neither can you, unless you remain in me.'
John 15:4

ALL   Come, Lord, fill us with your peace.

READER D   'May Christ dwell in your hearts through faith. . . . that you may be filled with all the fullness of God.'
Ephesians 3:17 and 19

ALL   Come, Lord, fill us with your peace.

HYMN   Peace is flowing like a river (HON)

ALTERNATIVES

HYMN   Lord of all hopefulness (HON)

READING   See Additional readings, number 5 (page 120)

PRAYERS   Your beautiful world is being spoilt today, dear God,
by our selfishness and greed.
Instead of peace there is discord and war.
Instead of love there is hatred and fear.
Help us, O Lord, to shut out of our individual lives
all that is selfish and greedy,
all hatred and bitterness.
Help us to have love and forgiveness in our hearts;
the desire to help others
and to share the good things of life.
Then, perhaps, if we learn to live
generously and peaceably as individuals
we shall become a generous and peaceful nation
and other nations will follow our example.
Amen.

See also assembly G52 or A1 (alternative prayer)

G59 Aliens and unsolved mysteries

HYMN   All people that on earth do dwell (HON/Source)

COMMENT   Our hymn has some interesting words to think about.

READER   All people that on *earth* do dwell . . .

COMMENT   Astronomers tell us that there are so many galaxies out in space, with billions of planets, that it is almost certain that there is life on other planets.

READER   . . . without our aid he did us make . . .

COMMENT   What if there is life on other planets? God the creator must have made them too. Did the Son of God live among them and save them?

READER   Romans 8:37-39

COMMENT   St Paul reassures us that even if there is life on other planets we have no need to fear, for nothing can separate us from the love of God.

PRAYER   Father Creator,
we are totally amazed
when we consider the vast size of your universe.
We believe that over millions of years
you created what we have and see today.
We do not know for sure,
but there may be other beings in other galaxies
made and saved by you.
If they exist, may they know and love you,
as we know and love you.
Bless all those who work hard
to extend our knowledge and appreciation
of your universe
and the whole of your amazing creation.
Amen.

HYMN   O the love of my Lord (HON)

ALTERNATIVES

HYMN   All the nations of the earth (HON)

PRAYERS   See assembly C24 or D27

G60 Fashion

HYMN	If I were a butterfly (HON)
COMMENT	Our opening hymn was about appreciating ourselves as we are, and not wanting to be something different.
SCRIPTURE READING	Matthew 1:4-6
COMMENT	This is the only description, in the Gospels, of what a person – in this case John – was wearing. That was because most people then were too poor to think or worry about fashion.
SCRIPTURE READING	Luke 12:22-28
COMMENT	Jesus said that we should not worry about clothes; life and love are much more important than what people wear.
PRAYER	Father Almighty, we can see and experience your love for us in the beauty of your creation. You have clothed our planet in the bright colours of nature. May we appreciate that while outward appearances are good, it is the quality of the life and love that they reveal which really matters. May our attraction for fashionable clothes not blind us to the more important need for a loving concern and respect for others in our lives. Amen.
HYMN	I watch the sunrise (HON)

ALTERNATIVES

HYMNS	Morning has broken (HON) All things bright and beautiful (HON/Source)

Additional readings

These readings may be used *ad lib.* according to the discretion of the reader.

1 Who has seen the wind, neither you nor I,
but when the trees hang down their heads
the wind is passing by.
Who has seen the wind, neither I nor you,
but when the leaves hang trembling,
the wind is passing through.
Christina Rossetti

2 In years gone by, the court jester was an important member of the king's household. By means of jokes and tricks he kept the king in good humour – and entertained the members of the royal household.

Some writer tells us what he believes to be the best retort any court jester gave. It was the retort given to his sovereign, a dictator who had the ancient 'power of life or death' over all his subjects, and it was supposed to be legally impossible for the king to change any sentence he passed on the subject. Becoming irritated by his court jester, in a sudden rage, the king sentenced him to death. Then, realising too late his rash decree, the king said to the court jester, 'In consideration of your faithful services, I will permit you to select the manner in which you prefer to die.' The court jester instantly answered, 'I select to die of old age.'
Anon

3 It is done. Once again the fire has penetrated the earth. Not with the sudden crash of thunderbolt ringing the mountain tops does the Master break down doors to enter his own home! Without earthquake or thunderclap, the flame has lit up the whole world from within. All things individually and collectively are penetrated and flooded by it, from the inmost core of the tiniest atom to the mighty sweep of the most universal laws of being. So naturally has it flooded every element, every energy, every connecting link in the unity of our cosmos, that one might suppose the cosmos to have burst spontaneously into flame.
Pierre Teilhard de Chardin

4 A great American storyteller wrote about two young people who were very much in love. Christmas Eve was coming and they wanted to give presents to one another. But they were very poor and had no money for presents. So each one, without telling the other, decided to sell his most precious possession. The girl's most precious possession was her long golden hair and she went to a hairdresser and had it cut off. She sold it then to buy a lovely watch chain for her lover's watch. He, meanwhile, had gone to a jeweller and sold his watch to buy two beautiful combs for his beloved's hair. Then they made their gifts. There were tears at first and then laughter. There was no hair for the combs and no watch for the watch chain. But there was something more precious and that was their self-sacrificing love for one another.

5 There is a huge statue of Christ holding a cross standing on the Andes, the mountain range between the countries of Argentine and Chile. The story of that statue is worth knowing.

Once Argentine and Chile were about to go to war with one another. They were quarrelling over some land which each said belonged to them. So both countries started to prepare for war. Then, on Easter Sunday, bishops in Argentine and Chile began to urge peace. They went round their countries crying out for peace in the name of Christ. The people did not want war and in the end they made their governments talk peace with one another, instead of war. The big guns, instead of being used for fighting, were melted down and made into the great big bronze statue of Christ. It now stands on the mountain between the two countries. Written on it are the words 'These mountains shall fall and crumble to dust before the people of Chile and Argentine shall forget their solemn covenant sworn at the feet of Christ.'
Maurice Nassan

6 Not merely in the words you say, not only in the deeds confessed,
but in the most unconscious way is Christ expressed.
Is it a very saintly smile? A holy light upon your brow?
Oh no! I felt his presence while you laughed just now.
For me, 'twas not the truth you taught, to you so clear, to me so dim;
but when you came, you straightway brought a sense of him.
So from your life he beckons me, and from your heart his love is shed,
till I lose sight of you, and see Christ instead.
Anon

120

7 Little Jesus, Lord of all,
cradled in the cattle stall,
swaddled safe, content to lay
Warm and wanted on the hay;
Mary with maternal joy
smiles upon her baby boy
sleeping, sated, laid to rest
from the fullness of her breast.

Anxious Joseph making sure
all is well and all secure,
his the ward and watch to keep,
bids the maiden mother sleep.

Ass and ox, with eyes intent,
gaze on them in wonderment,
careful lest their cramped tread
stir the infant in his bed.

All is quiet, all is peace;
hush, you world, your quarrels cease.
Watch with Joseph, vigil keeping,
for the Son of God is sleeping.
Killian Twell

8 A man went to stay with a friend in Cornwall, in a part where there were a large number of deep holes in the ground. These were disused mine shafts, some of which had no rails round them. He went for a walk one day and got lost. Darkness came and he realised that he was near these holes and it was dangerous to walk in the dark. But it was too cold to sit down and wait till morning so he walked on with great care. In spite of this, his feet slipped and he started to slide down a mine shaft. He managed to grasp a rock that was sticking out of the side of the shaft. There he hung, terrified, with his feet dangling. He managed to hang on for about twenty minutes, but the agony in his arms became so great that he knew he would soon have to let go and plunge to his death. He was about to let go when he saw, to his immense relief, a little light in the distance which began to grow greater and he knew that help was coming. He shouted loud with all the energy he had left. When the rescuers arrived and shone their light down on him, the first thing they saw was that his feet were dangling within a foot of solid earth. This mine shaft had been filled in! All his agony and fears had been for nothing.
Maurice Nassan

9 The cell was a concrete box too narrow to sit down in. One could only bend one's knees a little, so that they were thrust up against the door, and the position became so agonising that it was hard not to cry out. To pray in such circumstances was not easy, but it is a great and sweet solace if one can do so, and one must try with all one's strength to love more, not less. I had to struggle not to sink below the level of love and fall back into the realm of hatred, anger and revenge; to love Romulus Luca (the prison guard) not for a moment but continuously. I had to drive my soul to do this as one may push a vehicle with locked brakes. It was now that I came to understand Luca, his blindness and narrow hatred, his reactions which were like those of a dog rendered savage by being chained too long, or of a slave put in charge of slaves, with no freedom except to torment them. And then my thoughts went to those whom it was natural and easy to love. I found that now I loved them differently, now that I had learnt to love Luca. . . . And it was in that cell, my legs sticky with filth, that I at last came to understand the divinity of Jesus Christ, the most divine of all men, the one who had most deeply and intensely loved, and who had conceived the parable of the lost sheep.
Petru Dumitriu

10 I do not know so much the situation in the West because I have been away for such a long time – forty years. But now more and more there's this. Lenten raising of money to help the poorest. It's growing, and people are beginning to be more and more conscious that there are in the world people who are hungry and who are naked and who are sick and who have no shelter. And the rich want to share the hardship in some way just a little bit sometimes; the difficulty is that they don't give until it hurts. The new generation, especially the children, are understanding better. The children in England are making sacrifices to give a slice of bread to our children and the children of Denmark are making sacrifices to give a glass of milk to our children daily, and the children of Germany are making sacrifices to give one multi-vitamin daily to a child. These are the ways to greater love. These children when they grow up, they will have faith and love and a desire to serve and to give more!
Mother Teresa talking to Malcolm Muggeridge

11 Poverty is the moment in the world
when lilies and children
and all the things that matter,
don't.
It is the moment when only bread
is beautiful
because it means another hour or two
of living,
with only the hope that hope
is round the corner,
no idea or solution
from a perfect flower,
only live from day to day,
avoiding death.
Don't give a lily to a man like that.
If he is hungry enough,
he will eat it.
from *Young Scots Writing*

12 At that time there was neither non-existence nor existence; neither the worlds nor the sky, nor anything that is beyond. What covered everything, and where, and for whose enjoyment? Was there water unfathomable and deep? Death was not there, nor immortality; no knowing of night or day. That One Thing breathed without air, by its own strength; apart from it, nothing existed. Darkness was there, wrapped in yet more darkness; undistinguished, all this was one water; the incipient lay covered by the void. That One Thing became creative by the power of its own contemplation . . . the gods are later than this creative activity; who knows, then, from where this came into being? Where this creation came from, whether one supported it or not, He was supervising it from the highest heaven, He indeed knows; or He knows not!
Rig Veda 10, 29

13 In AD 1309 an Aztec Indian inhabitant of what is now Mexico City was found guilty of burning charcoal in the city and polluting the air. He was ordered to be hanged for the offence.

Today, Mexico City has a carbon-monoxide level greater than metropolitan New York, a sulphur-dioxide level greater than that of London, and ten times the industrial contaminants of the industrialised Rhine River valley.
John McLaughlin

14 Aristides, a non-Christian, defended the Christians before the Emperor Hadrian in the second century AD, in the following words:

'Christians love one another. They never fail to help widows. They save orphans from those who would hurt them. If a person has something, he gives freely to the person who has nothing. . . . This is really a new kind of person. There is something divine in them.'

15 The famous playwright, Dennis Potter, who wrote many plays for television, died of cancer in 1994, after a long illness. These words are from his last interview with Melvyn Bragg shortly before his death:

'I'm almost serene. I can celebrate life. Below my window there's an apple tree in blossom. It's white. And looking at it – instead of saying "Oh, that's a nice blossom" – now, looking at it through the window, I see the whitest, frothiest, bloomest blossom that there ever could be. The nowness of everything is absolutely wondrous. If you see the present tense – boy, do you see it, do you celebrate it!'

16 Laugh, laugh with joy. Lift up your hearts on high
for God is here, sharing our destiny.
We fight life's battles now with an ally.
Will you not hear the news, and laugh with me?
Be glad to give; be also glad to take
the gift of God, the giving and forgiving.
Give and accept, in joy that for our sake
the living God is here among the living.
John Ferguson

17 Our deepest fear is not that we are inadequate.
Our deepest fear is that we are powerful beyond measure.
It is our light, not our darkness, that most frightens us.
We ask ourselves, 'Who am I to be brilliant, gorgeous, talented, fabulous?'
Actually who are you not to be? You are a child of God.
Your playing small doesn't serve the world.
There's nothing enlightened about shrinking
so that other people won't feel insecure around you.

We are all meant to shine as children do.
We are born to manifest the glory of God that is within us.

It's not just in some of us;
it's in everyone.

And, as we let our own light shine,
we unconsciously give other people permission to do the same.
As we're liberated from our own fear,
our presence automatically liberates others.
Nelson Mandela

18 A big spider, which lived in the roof of an old house, decided to come and live a little lower down. So he spun a thread and came sliding down it and made a new web. He then began to catch flies and make himself fat, and because he became fat he also became very lazy and stupid. He was so pleased with himself one day as he was walking round his web and he looked up and saw the thread going up in the air. 'What's the use of that?' he said and he broke it. Immediately, he went crashing down with his web to the floor beneath and killed himself.
Maurice Nassan

19 A 15-year-old Bedouin boy named Muhammed adh-Dhib was searching for a stray goat in a desert region close to the Dead Sea, when he saw the opening of a small cave in a rocky cliff. He lazily threw a few stones through the hole and heard something break.

Thinking it might be hidden treasure, Muhammed ran back to camp and brought a friend, Ahmed Muhammed, to the cave. They squeezed through the opening into the cave and found among pieces of broken pottery, a number of clay cylinders, two feet high. Hoping for gold or precious stones the boys wrenched off the lids, but instead of the treasure they expected, they found only dark musty-smelling lumps of material. They were eleven scrolls made of thin strips of sheepskin sewn together, and coated in gummy, decomposed leather. More precious than gold, the Bible scrolls, hidden for nearly 1,900 years, are the oldest Bible manuscripts ever found. While the boys' families only received a few pounds from an Arab dealer, the world was enriched with a great religious treasure.
Anon

20   Dance over the mountains,
leap over the sea.
Take a message to Manuel
that he belongs to me.

Shu-Ping is in China,
Manuel is in Spain;
round the world spin a girdle bright,
and round the world again.

Joy and peace are the girdle,
love is the message we send;
you, Shu-Ping are my brother,
Manuel is my friend.

Bronya is sleeping in Poland,
Ranee's awake in Nepal;
sunshine and shadow divide us,
but God watches over us all.

Dance over the mountains,
leap over the sea.
Go and tell Lulu in Africa
that she belongs to me.
M. E. Rose

21   A tourist standing by Niagara Falls saw an eagle swoop upon a frozen lamb encased in a piece of floating ice. The eagle stood upon it and it drifted towards the rapids. Every now and then the eagle would proudly lift its head into the air to look around him, as much as to say, 'I am drifting on towards danger. I know what I am doing. I shall fly away and make good my escape before it is too late.' When he reached the edge, he stopped, spread his powerful wings, and leaped for flight; but alas, while he was feeding on the carcass, his feet had frozen to its fleece. He leaped and shrieked, and beat upon the ice with his wings until he went over into the chasm and darkness below.
Anon

22   There are words that are strangers to our experiences,
borrowed words – fashionable, off-the-rack, will-do words
that deceive us into believing
we have experienced their reality
but they don't dance, sing, cry, laugh,
smell of our journey –
they just sit there on the page.

Then there are words that have walked with us
and are intimate to our story –
words pregnant with the life of our experiences,
on fire, bloodied, luscious, simple,
rough-and-tumble, in tune words
that leap from the pages of our hearts
and tell in time ten thousand ways
the Great Story we each hold in trust.
Noel Davis

23   If you give a man a fish, he will eat once.
If you teach a man to fish, he will eat for the rest of his life.
If you are thinking a year ahead, plant a tree.
If you are thinking one hundred years ahead, educate the people.
By sowing seed, you will harvest once.
By planting a tree, you will harvest tenfold.
By educating the people, you will harvest one hundredfold.
Kuan-tzu (4th-3rd century BC)

24   In Rio, a group of Christians was working with street children. Every day boys from the street got together at one spot to chat, to discuss their problems and to share their fears and anger with one another. Many came regularly. The church people consisted of a Catholic priest, a Methodist, a priest of the Umbanda cult, a Presbyterian, and a young Lutheran pastor. One day one of the boys said, 'I would like to be baptised.'

'In which church, then?' asked the Catholic.

'Which church? In ours here, of course.'

'But to which church building would you like to go?'

'Building? No, to our church, here on the street. I want to be baptised here among us.'

The Methodist said he couldn't issue such a certificate. The Catholic thought it wouldn't be possible to perform jointly with the man from the Umbanda religion. The boy stuck to his wish.

Finally, the pastor organised the necessary things: he laid a board over two crates and filled an old boot with water for flowers, which the children provided. The Catholic brought along a candle. The baptism took place on the street, in the name of Jesus Christ.
Dorothee Soelle